Opening and Closing the Doors

THE URBAN INSTITUTE PRESS
2100 M Street, N.W.
Washington, D.C. 20037

Library of Congress Cataloging in Publication Data
Bean, Frank D.

Opening and Closing the Doors: Evaluating Immigration Reform and Control/Frank D. Bean, Georges Vernez, and Charles B. Keely.

1. Emigration and immigration law—United States. 2. Aliens, Illegal—United States. 3. Alien labor—United States. I. Vernez, Georges. II. Keely, Charles B. III. Title.

KF4819.B43 1989   342.73'082 [347.30282]   89-35240
                                                          CIP

ISBN 0-87766-429-3 (alk. paper)
ISBN 0-87766-428-5 (alk. paper; casebound)

Urban Institute books are printed on acid-free paper whenever possible.

Printed in the United States of America.

9 8 7 6 5 4 3

Distributed by:
          University Press of America
4720 Boston Way   3 Henrietta Street
Lanham, MD 20706   London WC2E 8LU ENGLAND

Opening and Closing the Doors

Evaluating Immigration Reform and Control

FRANK D. BEAN
GEORGES VERNEZ
CHARLES B. KEELY

RAND CORPORATION
Santa Monica, CA

THE URBAN INSTITUTE
Washington, DC

The RAND Corporation was chartered in 1948 as a nonprofit institution to "further and promote scientific, educational, and charitable purposes, all for the public welfare and security of the United States of America." To meet these objectives, RAND conducts rigorous analyses of significant national problems to provide decision-makers and the public with a better understanding of the policy issues involved.

RAND's research is analytic, objective, and interdisciplinary. National security programs focus on the planning, development, acquisition, deployment, support, and protection of military forces, and include international matters that may affect U.S. defense policy and strategy. Domestic programs include civil and criminal justice, education and human resources, health sciences, international economic studies, labor and population, and regulatory policies.

THE URBAN INSTITUTE is a nonprofit policy research and educational organization established in Washington, D.C., in 1968. Its staff investigates the social and economic problems confronting the nation and government policies and programs designed to alleviate such problems. The Institute has two goals for work in each of its research areas: to help shape thinking about societal problems and efforts to solve them, and to improve government decisions and performance by providing better information and analytic tools.

Through work that ranges from broad conceptual studies to administrative and technical assistance, Institute researchers contribute to the stock of knowledge available to public officials and private individuals and groups concerned with formulating and implementing more efficient and effective government policy.

ACKNOWLEDGMENTS

We are indebted to numerous persons who either generously provided comments on all or portions of the manuscript or otherwise provided assistance that contributed to its completion. They include Susan Gonzalez Baker, Harry Cross, Thomas Espenshade, Michael Fix, Lawrence Fuchs, Julie Goldsmith, Charles Kamasaki, Warren Leiden, Kevin McCarthy, Doris Meissner, Joyce Peterson, Lisa Roney, Felicity Skidmore, Alan Stapleton, Rick Swartz, and Wendy Zimmerman. Also, Jackie Bowen, LaVonia Proctor, and Terri Murray assisted with the production of the manuscript. Needless to say, the views and interpretations expressed here are our own and do not necessarily reflect the views of any of these individuals. Neither are these persons responsible for any errors that remain.

Conclusions or opinions expressed are those of the authors and do not necessarily reflect the views of other staff members, officers, trustees, or advisory groups of either the RAND Corporation or The Urban Institute, or any organizations that provide either of them with financial support.

CONTENTS

FOREWORD

Large-scale immigration has always been part of the American experience. The United States has been seen as a place of opportunity for immigrants. And immigration has been seen as providing benefits to the nation. But Americans can also be ambivalent about immigration, an ambivalence that typically centers on concern about jobs. The most recent such period, beginning in the early 1970s, culminated a decade and a half later in passage of the 1986 Immigration Reform and Control Act (IRCA). This Yearbook, the first of several, provides the context within which the effects of IRCA—the most sweeping immigration legislation to be passed for more than twenty years—can be evaluated.

One of the main goals of IRCA's sponsors was to reduce illegal immigration. But congressional compromises, providing striking testimony to public ambivalence on the issue, expanded IRCA's focus to include changes in employment, agricultural labor, civil rights, and federal reimbursement policies and programs. IRCA touches most aspects of American life. As such it is important that policymakers understand its implications, and the implications of further changes Congress is considering just three years after IRCA's passage.

To undertake the task of interpreting IRCA in the wider context of shifting U.S. immigration patterns, the Program for Research on Immigration Policy was established in 1988 by the RAND Corporation and The Urban Institute. The Ford Foundation provided initial core funding.

Our institutions are pleased to be part of this major effort. Our participation reflects each of our organization's continuing commitment to the study of immigration issues and demographic issues more generally. These are important public policy issues. The nation's ability to respond to demographic realities will influence how well it can remain competitive in a global economy and still meet the needs of its dependent populations at home, without overburdening the generation that bears the cost.

This Yearbook—a joint product of RAND and The Urban Institute—is the first of many contributions that the Program for Research on Immigration Policy will make to the immigration literature. In addition to subsequent Yearbooks, the Program plans to publish conference volumes and several series of papers. We are confident that this body of work will contribute to informing the policy debate about an important aspect of our society.

William Gorham
President
The Urban Institute

David Lyon
Vice President
The RAND Corporation

PREFACE

After a lull lasting more than 40 years, immigration to the United States began to increase considerably in the late 1960s after the passage of the 1965 Amendments to the Immigration and Nationality Act of 1952. By giving priority to family reunification as a basis for immigrant admission, these amendments led to rates of immigration that by historical standards were, and are, quite high. If estimates of undocumented entrants are included, levels of immigration have approached in recent years the record figures that occurred in the early part of the 20th century. In fiscal year 1988, more than 640,000 immigrants were admitted for lawful permanent residence in the United States. After allowing for estimated departures and for illegal entrants (estimated at 200,000 per year), immigration accounted for almost a third of the country's population growth in that year.

The last 20 years have witnessed other changes in immigration as well. The ethnic composition of legal immigrants has shifted away from a preponderance of Europeans to a preponderance of Asians and Latin Americans. The Hispanic element in the recent immigration flows has also been supplemented by sizeable numbers of refugees from Cuba and by a substantial number of undocumented migrants from Mexico. Immigrants are thus not only greater in number than at any time since the early 1920s, but perhaps also more visible than at any time in the nation's history. And to many lawmakers and citizens during the early 1980s, the nation's immigration policy appeared ineffectual in curtailing illegal immigration at the same time that it kept tens of thousands of legal petitioners from obtaining entry visas. Such concerns resulted in a strong movement to change immigration law.

After several narrow defeats reflecting continuing controversy, this movement nonetheless resulted in the passage of IRCA in November of 1986. This legislation is the most sweeping revision of U.S. immigration policy since 1965 when the national origins quota system was abolished. IRCA contains several major provisions: a legalization program; provisions about employer requirements and sanctions; antidiscrimination provisions; a program to reimburse states for added costs due legalization; a program of welfare applicant screening to determine migration status and eligibility; and a variety of agricultural provisions.

Objective, nonpartisan evaluations and assessments of IRCA and its effects are essential for future deliberations about U.S. policies for the regulation of immigration and the treatment of immigrants for several reasons. First, such research efforts might help to reduce dissension over immigration issues. Second, they will inform congressional decisionmaking over the possible "sunsetting" of IRCA's employer sanctions and nondiscrimation provisions that are to be initially reviewed in late 1989 and early 1990. Third, such research will inform the important policy decisions the law assigns to IRCA's administering agencies. These range from such diverse issues as developing the criteria for, and size of, the Replenishment Agricultural Worker (RAWs) labor force to the amount of "impact" grants distributed to the states. Finally, the research will provide an assessment of the degree to which IRCA's success or failure can be ascribed to either the law's *design* or its *implementation*—an assessment that should be central to future reform initiatives, such as those embodied in the currently proposed Simpson–Kennedy reforms pertaining to legal immigration.

To conduct such research, as well as to study immigration more generally, the RAND Corporation and The Urban Institute in February 1988 established jointly the Program for Research on Immigration Policy. The Program is dedicated to supporting the formulation of immigration and immigrant policies at the state and national levels and in relevant areas of the private sector. The main objectives of the Program are to study the important domestic and international issued raised by the Immigration Reform and Control Act (IRCA) of 1986; to address the larger, continuing questions and problems of immigration policy; and to disseminate and exchange information about IRCA and immigration through publications and conferences. Achieving these goals will contribute significantly to the national understanding of IRCA and immigration as well as provide findings relevant for future policy formulation and revisions. The present volume contributes to achieving these objectives.

Victor H. Palmieri
Chair, Advisory Board,
Program for Research on Immigration Policy

INTRODUCTION

Over the past 25 years, patterns of immigration to the United States have changed dramatically. During the 1970s and early 1980s increasing numbers of immigrants and refugees came to this country, along with an increasing number of illegal immigrants. These changes inspired a movement to reassess and reform U.S. immigration policy. Reflecting this concern at the highest levels of government, in 1978 the U.S. Congress established the Select Commission on Immigration and Refugee Policy to review the nation's immigration policies and to make recommendations for their modification. In its final report, the commission concluded that "one issue has emerged as most pressing—that of undocumented/illegal migration" (Select Commission on Immigration and Refugee Policy, 1981:35).

In October 1986 Congress adopted the Immigration Reform and Control Act (IRCA), which instituted the most sweeping changes in U.S. immigration law since 1965. In keeping with many of the final recommendations of the Select Commission on Immigration and Refugee Policy (1981), IRCA included several provisions designed to reduce the number of illegal immigrants coming to and residing in the United States. Unlike the commission's proposals, however, which recommended the modification of certain aspects of legal immigration policy (including several of the preference categories), IRCA left legal immigration policy largely unaffected, although some of the law's provisions, most notably the legalization programs, provided for substantial increases in legal immigration.

In 1989, more than a decade after creation of the Select Commission and nearly three years since passage of IRCA, Congress is considering further changes in immigration policy, including modifications in legal immigration policy and limitations on the total number of refugees and immigrants granted permanent resident alien status each year. It is time to try to gain some perspective on the nature and basic direction of recent changes in U.S. immigration patterns and policies, especially as they have been affected by IRCA.

It would be naive to think this an easy task. Clearly, thorough scrutiny of the legislation contained in IRCA and of its implementation is integral to any examination of U.S. immigration and immigration policy. But there are divergent interpretations of the political intent of the legislation and of its potential impact. The task is further complicated by the possibility that IRCA's implementation may not lead to the effects it was intended to generate; indeed, its unanticipated consequences may prove even more important than its intended effects. It is thus important to study the actual effects of the legislation. Although insufficient time has elapsed since the passage of IRCA for all its effects to be felt, enough time has passed to begin the examination. Moreover, the significance of IRCA can be most clearly understood by considering the broader context of shifting U.S. immigration patterns and policies both before and after enactment of the law.

To understand IRCA's implementation process and outcomes—as well as to study more generally the significant policy questions pertaining to U.S. immigration—the RAND Corporation and The Urban Institute established in 1988 the Program for Research on Immigration Policy, with initial support from the Ford Foundation. The Program will follow the process of IRCA over its five-year implementation period, as well as investigate broader continuing issues relevant to immigration and immigration policy. Among other activities, the Program is committed to publishing an annual series of overviews on contributions of the Program, other work in the area, and policy developments.

The overarching purpose of this document, the first in this series, is to outline the general immigration trends and policy proposals that constitute the lens through which IRCA and other recently proposed changes in U.S. immigration policy must be viewed. The specific purposes are: (1) to outline the major historical features of immigration to the United States; (2) to examine in detail the provisions, implementation, and effects of IRCA; and (3) to review recent trends in legal immigration and refugee admissions to the United States, together with recent proposals to alter legal immigration policy.

Chapter 1 in this study briefly reviews the history of U.S. immigration as background for the rest of this undertaking. Chapter 2 looks at current U.S. immigration policy and highlights the issues that led to IRCA's passage. Chapter 3 examines the major provisions of IRCA. Chapter 4 assesses progress to date in implementing the programs mandated by IRCA. Chapter 5 discusses the outcomes that can be measured to date. Chapter 6 examines whether illegal immigration seems to have been curtailed by passage of IRCA. Chapter 7 presents data on recent trends in legal immigration and refugee flows in order to provide a context for examining current proposals to modify the nation's laws with respect to legal immigration. Chapter 8 concludes the study by moving beyond IRCA and a strictly legislative focus. It suggests the need to explore the meaning of immigration and its place in American life by addressing immigrant integration in relation to the U.S. economy and labor market and foreign policy. These are among the many issues that impinge on the migration patterns of hundreds of thousands of people from other lands who still seek to make the United States their home and the home of their children.

Chapter One

HISTORICAL CONTEXT

The United States is often characterized as "a nation of immigrants." It has also been seen as a place of economic opportunity for immigrants, as vividly conveyed by the phrase "the golden door".[1] Entry through the "golden door" has historically promised access to the economic opportunities enjoyed by a country with vast natural resources and, throughout much of its history, an open and expanding frontier. Now as the United States moves into the last decade of the 20th century, the question has arisen of whether the country is undergoing a changed outlook on immigration.

OUTLOOKS ON IMMIGRATION

Immigration has not only been seen as conferring opportunity on immigrants. It has also been viewed as providing benefits, especially labor benefits, for the nation. But even as the country has welcomed large numbers of new immigrants, Americans have often remained ambivalent about immigration. As the nation moved into periods of slower economic growth in the early 1970s, many citizens expressed concern that the nation's resources, especially its economic resources as represented by jobs, might not be sufficient to absorb the numbers of immigrants arriving on American shores. Similar worries had emerged before, especially early in the 20th century, when the greatest volume of immigration in the history of the United States occurred. Restrictionist pressures eventually resulted in passage of the National Origins Quota Act of 1924, which substantially curtailed the flow of immigration to the country.

One may ask whether the nation is now entering a new era with respect to its immigration policies. In October 1986 the U.S. Congress passed the Immigration Reform and Control Act (IRCA), which was signed into law by President Ronald Reagan on November 6 of that year (U.S. Congress, 1986). It is too early to discern completely the significance of this legislation. Only a careful monitoring of IRCA's implementation and effects, together with a close examination of post-IRCA developments in immigration policy, will make clear whether this legislation marks the beginning of a new direction in national immigration policy. IRCA may represent, on the one hand, the first step in an effort to restrict immigration levels. On the other hand, it may be viewed as an effort to legalize and regularize immigration, thus fostering conditions that may help to preserve current and even allow for increased levels of legal immigration and to reinforce inclusive orientations in American society.

The restrictionist perspective interprets IRCA's passage as part of a process of "closing the back door before trying to close the front door" (Lamm and Ihmhoff, 1985; Stein, 1989). According to this viewpoint, it was impossible to consider proposals to modify the nation's policies with respect to legal immigration while thousands of undocumented workers were crossing the nation's borders illegally. The situation in which petitioners for legal entry were waiting years in backlogs to obtain visas, while others were entering the country illegally and seemingly with impunity, constituted an inequity that many observers found intolerable. For those wishing to curb both illegal and legal immigration, IRCA represents a necessary first step in restricting legal immigration.

The second of these two perspectives, however, interprets recent changes in U.S. immigration policy, especially the passage of IRCA, as a process consisting of "closing the back door while keeping the front door open" (Fuchs, 1987; forthcoming). In this view, the provisions of IRCA aimed at curtailing illegal immigration constitute an effort to close the back door, while the fact that IRCA left legal immigration largely unaffected, and even provided for increases in legal immigration through its various legalization programs and through other minor changes (such as advancing the eligibility date for the registry program from 1948 to 1972), constitute an effort to keep the front door open, and even to open it more widely. These changes, in helping to reduce the size of an exploitable worker underclass and in providing pathways to permanent residency and citizenship in the United States, have served to bring a large group of persons under the full protection of the U.S. Constitution (Fuchs, 1987; forthcoming).

Further changes in immigration policy over the next few years may provide an indication of which of these two viewpoints more accurately describes the current direction of U.S. immigration policy. For example, if any subsequent changes in legal immigration policy do not reduce the number of legal immigrants below current levels, then the second perspective might be deemed more accurate. If, on the other hand, laws are enacted that substantially reduce legal immigration, observers might come to view the first perspective as more accurate. Recent legislative events seem to point in the former direction. On July 13, 1989 the U.S. Senate approved, by a vote of 81 to 17, a major revision of U.S. legal immigration policy (we discuss this bill [the Kennedy-Simpson bill, S.358] and other proposals in chapter 7). Although the bill establishes a loose ceiling of 630,000 visas annually, the level is sufficiently high that it would be hard to call the legislation restrictionist. Before the measure can become law, however, the U.S. House of Representatives must also act. Whatever the final outcome, differences in perspective and outlook concerning the impact and meaning of continued immigration to the United States are likely to persist.

HISTORICAL CONTEXT

Many Americans in the post-World War II era may have thought that large-scale immigration was part of the country's distant past.[2] Laws passed in the 1920s curtailed immigration sharply, and the economic downturn resulting from the depression reduced even the remaining flow to a trickle. The decade and a half from about 1927 to 1942, however, turned out to be the exception rather than the rule. The immigration flows that have occupied the nation's attention the past decade had their origins in trends that began over four decades ago. These trends underscore the continuity of large-scale migration as part of the American experience.

Some of the trends began in 1942 in the midst of World War II when the United States and Mexico adopted the Bracero Program of "temporary workers" in agriculture. Before this program ended in 1964, it brought in over 100,000 workers per year (over 400,000 annually in the peak years of the late 1950s). Many of those involved in it stayed permanently, but even those who returned home influenced the U.S. economy and society during their temporary stays. Perhaps the most significant legacy of the Bracero Program for the country was that what was thought to be mostly temporary migration often turned into permanent immigration.

After World War II, America also began formally to accept refugees in large numbers. The groups admitted under the Displaced Persons Act of 1948 and the Refugee Relief Act of 1953, along with Hungarians in 1956, Cubans beginning in 1959, and Indochinese starting in 1975, were only the most conspicuous of the many refugee groups admitted for permanent settlement in a series of ad hoc decisions separate from ordinary immigration law. In addition, legal immigration resumed its growth.

These general trends make clear that immigration in the post–World War II era continued to be an integral part of American society, not merely part of the country's past. U.S. history has witnessed a series of immigrant waves, the troughs usually marked by wars and steep declines in the U.S. economy. What has made each wave unique are the different countries involved and the distinct characteristics of the immigrants themselves. (Figure 1.1 presents the official data series on immigrants admitted for permanent residence beginning in 1820, the year in which immigrants were first counted.)

The initial waves of immigrants came to the East Coast of the United States. British, Scots, and Scotch Irish of colonial times consisted mainly of two groups—unattached and unemployed males, frequently indentured, and family groups who took up farming, eventually owning the land they tilled (Bailyn, 1986). Irish peasants fleeing famine and landlessness began to arrive in the first half of the 19th century, although the great Irish migrations occurred later, after the worst of the potato famines. They usually abandoned agriculture and settled in the expanding urban centers of America or provided the muscle power to develop canals and railroads, the first extensive public works programs in the United States. Although many Germans had come earlier, sizable numbers of German peasants also came during this time, as did a few political radicals of the failed 1848 political rebellions in Europe.

After the American Civil War, more Germans followed, plus British and Scandanavian immigrants displaced by the industrial revolution and by land shortages stemming from the combined effects of rapid population growth and inheritance laws in Europe. Many of them settled the farms of the Middle West and populated the urban settlements that became the industrial heartland of America. In the 1880s the immigrants from northern Europe began to be supplanted by immigrants from southern and eastern Europe. These latter constituted the greatest wave yet, peaking at over 10 million entrants in the decade before World War I (1905–1914) and continuing into the 1920s.

Figure 1.1 LEGAL IMMIGRATION

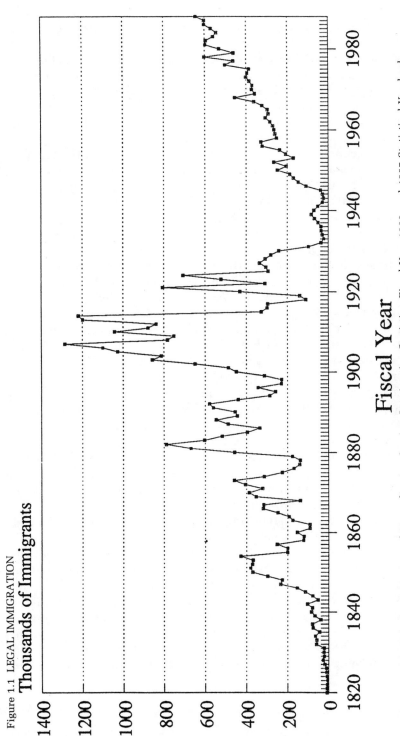

Source: United States Immigration and Naturalization Service. *Immigration Statistics: Fiscal Year 1988.* and *1987 Statistical Yearbook of the Immigration and Naturalization Service.* pp. 1–5.

Chinese men were recruited beginning in the late 1840s to provide labor in Hawaii and California (and other territory annexed from Mexico) and to build the railroads of the West. This migration continued until racism and opposition to the competition from low-cost imported labor from China resulted in its prohibition in the 1880s. Japanese and Filipinos successively took their place, until Japanese entry was curtailed by the Gentlemen's Agreement of 1907. Asians were not only ineligible for citizenship, a strategy that was used to try to guarantee that they would only stay temporarily, but their entry generally was forbidden as part of a series of race-conscious laws to control immigration beginning in 1917. Along the southern border of the United States, Mexicans moved freely into the United States, increasing their levels of immigration especially after 1880 as the Southwest developed economically. Their labor opened mines, such as the copper mines in Arizona, and built and maintained the railroads of the Southwest (Bean and Tienda, 1988).

The most recent wave of immigration began with Mexican temporary laborers of the World War II era (not included in the statistics in figure 1.1 because they were not admitted as permanent residents) and postwar European refugees. The ending of national origin quotas in 1965, which operated to favor European immigration, added to the new wave by opening opportunities for Asians. The immigration preference system was extended to the Western Hemisphere by two related laws in 1976 and 1978, which put subsequent Western Hemisphere immigration on the same footing as immigration from the Eastern Hemisphere.

The new influx was not restricted only to legal immigration. The ending of the Bracero Program in 1964 did not eliminate labor demand in the United States. Many workers who came legally under the Bracero Program now came illegally, doing what they had always done, journeying North for work. And illegal migration was not limited to Mexicans. Many Europeans, Caribbean islanders, and migrants from Latin, Asian, and African countries also came illegally, because obtaining an immigrant visa involved long waits or was impossible under the post-1965 immigration policies. Some returned and some stayed. Some undocumented migrants eventually found a way, through marriage, education, or work experience, to qualify for legal status and to regularize their presence under prevailing immigration law. Undocumented workers were found in jobs outside agriculture and far from the Southwest, including some even at work refurbishing the Statue of Liberty. Illegal migration became a national issue.

Since 1965 the United States has been attempting to cope with the post–World War II wave of immigrants. The increasing numbers, shifting national origins, and sometimes illegal status of the immigrants were unexpected and constituted a source of disturbance for some Americans. Many commentators suggested that the country had lost control of its borders and that illegal migration had to be curtailed [for examples of such views, see Bean and Sullivan (1985)]. Continued refugee flows involving new groups seemed to reduce the degree of compassion that could be devoted to each successive group. The change in the national origins of immigrants received less attention than did their numbers, owing perhaps to heightened sensitivities resulting from the civil rights movement. Yet the broad response to calls for a Constitutional amendment to make English the national language (successful state referenda were on the November 1988 ballots of Arizona, Colorado and Florida) suggests that concerns about ethnic success and linguistic diversity have been rising in the public consciousness.

Pressures mounted to curtail illegal immigration. These manifested themselves in several years of congressional debate, culminating in 1986 in the passage of the Immigration Reform and Control Act (IRCA). Many of IRCA's provisions had a long history. This was especially true of employer sanctions. On February 5, 1952, Senator Paul Douglas, of Illinois, introduced during Senate floor debate, an amendment to the 1952 Immigration and Nationality Act to provide for penalties against employers of illegal aliens (this was defeated 69 to 12). In 1971, Congressman Peter W. Rodino, of New Jersey, had also introduced legislation to restrict the hiring of undocumented aliens.[3] By the time the legislation passed, many of its key provisions had been thoroughly considered and debated over many years.

PREVIOUS POLICY PERIODS

How do those broad trends divide themselves in terms of policy periods? The nation's immigration policies may be grouped roughly into three periods (Cafferty et al., 1983). The first is the period before 1875, when minimal restrictions applied to the admission of immigrants to the United States. The Alien and Sedition Acts, passed in 1789, established the first federal statutory limit on immigration, although the presidential powers authorized by the act to expel dangerous persons from the country were apparently never used, and Congress failed to renew the act in 1800. Various pieces of legislation during the period also had minor effects on who was allowed to enter, but the nation was not to devote much attention to immigration until after the Civil War, when three developments occurred: in 1870 the Civil Rights Act was passed guaranteeing equal protection under the law for aliens; in 1874 the U.S. Supreme Court ruled that states had the right to permit aliens to vote; and in a major ruling in 1876, the Court held that regulation of immigration was a federal prerogative under the Interstate Commerce clause of the U.S. Constitution.

The second major period of U.S. immigration policy extended from 1875 to 1965, during which time the country's policies were increasingly governed by restrictionist criteria. At various times, laws were passed that were designed to exclude undesirable aliens, such as legislation in 1875 and 1885 that barred contract laborers and operated to prohibit disproportionately the entrance of persons from Asian countries. In the early 1920s pressures mounted to restrict immigration on the basis of national origin, and in 1924 the National Origins Quota Act was passed by Congress. The act established quotas based on the ethnic ancestry of the U.S. population in 1920. During World War II, Congress in 1943 repealed the policy of Chinese exclusion and after the war attempted to facilitate the entry of refugees (passing the Displaced Persons Act in 1948 and its amendment in 1950). During this time, the earlier-mentioned Bracero Program also was in effect as an instrument to relieve labor shortages in agriculture in the American Southwest. Essentially, however, the restrictionist orientation of U.S. policy continued, including its reaffirmation in the McCarren-Walter Immigration Act of 1952.

The third major period of U.S. immigration policy extends from 1965 to the present. In 1965, amendments to the 1952 Immigration and Nationality Act were passed that abolished the national origins quota system and established kinship ties with U.S. citizens or resident aliens as the dominant criteria for obtaining immigration visas. This emphasis on family reunification in legal immigration policy remains in effect to the present, although proposals for its modification have recently passed in the Senate, as mentioned earlier, and are under consideration in the House of Representatives.

Two major problems that the nation's post–World War II immigration policies did not deal with effectively, at least until the 1980s, concerned refugees and illegal aliens. The former was addressed in the Refugee Act of 1980, which we discuss in chapter 7. And, of course, the matter of illegal immigration is one of the major focuses of the Immigration Reform and Control Act of 1986. As noted previously, it remains unclear whether the United States is entering a new era in immigration policy. To begin to address this question, the next chapter provides a more detailed description of current immigration policy.

Notes

1. This latter description of immigrant passage is used in the title of at least two recent books on U.S. immigration (Cafferty et al., 1983; Reimers, 1985).

2. For discussions of the history of immigration to and immigration policy in the United States, see Auerbach and Harper (1973), Bennet (1963), Cafferty et al. (1983), Divine (1957), Higham (1955), Hutchinson (1981), Muller and Espenshade (1985), and Reimers (1985).

3. IRCA is also referred to as the Simpson-Rodino Act, after Senator Alan Simpson of Wyoming, Republican Whip, and Congressman Peter W. Rodino, past chairman of the House Judiciary Committee and a longtime leader on immigration issues who retired from Congress at the end of 1988.

Chapter Two

CURRENT IMMIGRATION POLICY

Immigration policy refers to the laws and practices that accomplish two related but distinct goals:

☐ To allow persons to reside in the United States permanently (including refugees admitted for resettlement), with the right to petition voluntarily to become citizens; and

☐ To permit persons to enter the United States and stay for varying but limited lengths of time, without the right to petition for citizenship.

The first goal refers to *immigrants* as usually defined: people who come to settle, live, and work in a new homeland and usually, but not necessarily, to become citizens in due course. The second objective refers to a variety of people who enter with some temporary status: tourists, students, people on business trips, and temporary workers of all sorts—agricultural laborers, athletes, entertainers, managers in multinational corporations, media representatives, diplomats, exchange visitors working in research centers and government laboratories, and scientists in medicine, industry and universities. The distinction between permanent immigrants and aliens on temporary status (for example workers or visitors) is not always clear given that as many as one-third of those admitted as immigrants return eventually to their homelands (Warren and Peck, 1980) and given that many visitors overstay the authorized durations of their visas, some never returning to their countries of origin.

The majority of temporary entrants are tourists who leave within six months of admission. In 1987, for example, 8.9 million (or 72 percent) of the 12.3 million people admitted for temporary stays in the United States were "visitors for pleasure," or tourists. Some of the other 3.4 million entrants stay for longer periods (like students) and even work legally during their stay in the United States (like managers in U.S. multinationals). All, however, have stays that are limited to a specific purpose and time period.

If they qualify, nonimmigrants are permitted to adjust their status to that of permanent resident alien. In 1987, for example, 36 percent of the 601,516 people granted permanent resident status were in the United States already and adjusted their status while here (U.S. Immigration and Naturalization Service, 1988a). Moreover, even this figure is an underestimate because others already in the United States, some illegally, went to their home countries to pick up their immigrant visas at a U.S. embassy. Such immigrants are not included in the count as adjusting their status, but appear in official statistics as new entrants.

In describing current U.S. immigration policy, this document's discussion emphasizes permanent resident aliens. It should be remembered, however, that a complicated system of temporary admissions often leads to adjustments of status, so that the usual policy focus on permanent immigration becomes somewhat fuzzy. Later sections of this document refer to the interplay between temporary and permanent migration, and to the need to distinguish the two processes when considering policies that are responsive to the needs and realities of international population movements of all types.

CURRENT IMMIGRATION AND REFUGEE POLICY

U.S. immigration policy has four broad objectives:

☐ To reunite families of citizens and legal permanent residents;
☐ To admit needed workers, some as permanent residents and some for temporary stays;
☐ To resettle those of the world's refugees who are of special interest to the United States for foreign or domestic policy reasons, or for humanitarian reasons because of their suffering and the desperation of their situation; and
☐ To accommodate the temporary stays of a variety of people, from tourists to diplomats, whose movement across borders is part of the political, economic, and social practice of most contemporary societies.

These four objectives are achieved by granting visas to foreign nationals for permanent residence or temporary stays. Permanent residence (with the right to apply for citizenship, usually after five years of residence) implies an important commitment and benefit granted by the country of destination. The complexity of the law and the bureaucratic attention paid to applications are understandably greater for permanent resident status than for temporary status. But the latter is by no means always easily granted, especially in the case of countries where temporary visa holders tend to remain illegally in the United States in large numbers.

Immigrants can qualify for entry in one of four categories: (1) immediate relatives of adult U.S. citizens (spouse, children, and parents); (2) other relatives of U.S. citizens and the spouses and unmarried children of permanent residents; (3) needed workers or persons in the arts or professions, or in occupations in short supply; and (4) refugees and asylees.

The first track reflects the current emphasis in U.S. immigration law that an adult citizen should be able to be joined by a spouse, children, and parents, without delays beyond those necessary to process applications and perform checks to prevent fraud.[1] In fiscal year (FY) 1987, when 601,516 people became permanent immigrants, 36 percent were immediate relatives of citizens. Of these immediate relatives, 61 percent were spouses, 18 percent were children, and 21 percent were parents of the sponsoring U.S. citizens. A recent U.S. General Accounting Office (GAO) study reported that 64 percent of the petitions on behalf of immediate relatives of U.S. citizens were made by native-born Americans (not by naturalized citizens) (GAO, 1988a). In short, about one in four of all current legal immigrants are immediate relatives of native-born U.S. citizens. Most of these relatives of U.S. citizens are from countries where the United States has a large military presence including Germany, Korea, England, Japan, and the Philippines (Jasso and Rosenzweig, 1986), underscoring the importance of military marriages as a cause of immigration to this country.

The second and third immigrant tracks—the second involving other relatives of citizens and spouses and unmarried children of permanent residents, and the third involving needed workers or persons in the arts or professions—are limited to 270,000 visas a year. The structure of the law reflects the correct assumption that demand will outstrip supply for these visas, so they are distributed according to a set of six preferences (table 2.1). In addition, the law prescribes that no more than 20,000 of the 270,000 visas can be used by natives of a single country. For those applying for an occupational preference (the third and sixth preferences in table

Table 2.1 WORLDWIDE LIMITED IMMIGRANTS (270,000 ANNUALLY)

Preference	Provision	Percentage and Number of Visas
First	Unmarried adult sons and daughters of U.S. citizens	20%, or 54,000
Second	Spouses and unmarried sons and daughters of permanent resident aliens	26%, or 70,200[a]
Third	Members of the professions of exceptional ability and their sons and daughters	10%, or 27,000[a]
Fourth	Married sons and daughters of U.S. citizens and their spouses and children	10%, or 27,000[a]
Fifth	Brothers and sisters of U.S. citizens (at least 21 years of age) and their children	24%, or 64,800[a]
Sixth	Workers in skilled or unskilled occupations in which laborers are in short supply in the United States and their spouses and children	10%, or 27,000[a]
Nonpreference	Other qualified applicants	Any numbers not used above

a. Numbers not used in higher preferences may be used in these categories.
Source: U.S. Immigration and Naturalization Service. 1983. *1982 Statistical Yearbook of the Immigration and Naturalization Service.*

2.1), the law also requires an individual labor certification that no U.S. worker is available with the requisite skills. This certification further requires that the terms of the job offered not undercut prevailing U.S. wages and conditions.

The limited number of annual visas available to achieve these family reunion and employment goals, together with the 20,000 ceiling on per-country use, has led to backlogs in some of the categories, requiring many applicants to wait several years before immigrant visas are granted to them. For example, the U.S. State Department reported a backlog of 402,221 in the second preference and 1,469,231 in the fifth preference as of January 1989.[2] Backlogs are concentrated in a few countries of high demand, including Mexico, Korea, India, and the Philippines. Throughout U.S. history, immigration flows usually have been dominated by three or four countries in any given decade, although the set of countries has changed over time. Irish, Germans, and British dominated before the Civil War. Italians, along with Slavs and Jews from eastern Europe and Russia, dominated in the heyday of immigration around the turn of the century. Today, Mexicans, Filipinos, Koreans, and Southeast Asian refugees represent high proportions of immigrant entrants.

The fourth immigrant track—that of refugees admitted for permanent residence—is determined annually by a process mandated by the 1980 Refugee Act. The president (through the coordinator for refugees in the State Department) consults the Senate and the House Committee on the Judiciary about the overall number of refugees and the regions of the world containing refugees whose resettlement is deemed by the president to be of special humanitarian interest to the United States.[3] The refugee coordinator on behalf of the president then submits a report to the U.S. Congress on the world refugee situation, detailing the numbers proposed for resettlement and why the admission of such people is of special interest. Mechanisms also exist for emergency consultations by the president if an unforeseen event develops meriting additional refugees.

The 1980 Refugee Act brought the U.S. legal definition of refugees into conformity with international law, to which the United States had acceded by signing the 1967 United Nations Protocol on the Status of Refugees. The 1980 Act also codified other refugee-related policy, such as specifying special entitlements for refugees to aid their integration into the workforce and society. From the end of World War II to 1980, refugee admissions had been left at the discretion of the president.

From 1981 to 1988, these tracks to permanent residence generated about 540,000 to 600,000 legal immigrants yearly. About 32 percent of these were immediate relatives of U.S. citizens, about 46 percent entered under the numerically limited categories covered by the preference system, about 18 percent were refugees and asylees adjusting their status, and less than 4 percent fell into various other special immigrant categories (ministers of religion, employees of the U.S. government abroad, retired employees of international organizations, and so on). In considering overall levels of immigration to the United States, it is important to remember that the number of immigrants entering the country every year exceeds the number who actually settle permanently here. Many immigrants decide not to stay in the United States for a variety of reasons. Recent estimates indicate that about 30 percent of all "permanent" immigrants eventually leave the United States (Jasso and Rosenzweig, 1986; Warren and Peck, 1980). Some native-born U.S. citizens also emigrate for a variety of work and retirement reasons. Thus, the number of people who become permanent resident aliens each year is only part, although a very important part, of the story on net migration to the United States.

WHAT LED TO IRCA?

This overview of current immigration policy sets the stage for considering some of the specific issues that led to passage of the Immigration Reform and Control Act (IRCA) in October 1986. To a considerable degree, although not entirely, the law was a response to a perception that illegal immigration was increasingly becoming a problem. But as we have noted, IRCA and its provisions are only one segment of the picture of recent changes and proposed revisions in U.S. immigration policy. As we describe in chapter 7, substantial congressional activity has already occurred since IRCA's passage, and more seems likely.

In 1964 the United States terminated the Bracero Program with Mexico that had operated since 1942. Public opposition to conditions of life for migrant workers (as reflected in the title of Edward R. Murrow's television documentary "Harvest of Shame"), the civil rights movement, and effective lobbying by labor, church, and ethnic groups culminated in congressional refusal to continue the program. Increased illegal entry resulted almost immediately, because economic incentives among employers and workers and patterns of temporary migration had become too deeply entrenched to change overnight. Importantly for employers in the United States, immigration law at the time specifically exempted the employment of undocumented or illegal aliens from the category of illegal acts. U.S. law declared that it was illegal for an alien to take a job without proper documents but not illegal for an employer to hire an undocumented migrant.

In addition to illegal Mexican immigration, some illegal immigration also occurred from other countries. The Immigration Act of 1965 ended the national origins quotas that had allocated visas in proportion to the national origin representation of the population already in the United States. Since the quota system had favored mainly northern and western European countries, the 1965 act led to substantial changes in the origin distribution of immigrant visas. Although the demand for emigration from Europe to the United States declined considerably during this time because of European economic prosperity, some immigrants from those countries found it difficult to get an immigrant visa. To circumvent this difficulty, some came as tourists or on other types of nonimmigrant visas and simply stayed and worked, the Irish being the most recent and conspicuous example. Others simply crossed the border (frequently the Canadian border) and went to work illegally. In addition to Mexicans and some Europeans, entry by undocumented aliens and visa violations involving persons from other countries (by taking unauthorized work or staying beyond allotted visa periods) contributed to growing illegal migration.

Speculations put forth during the 1970s about the size of the illegal population resident in the United States varied widely, even among government sources, although it was clear that some regions of the country were more affected than others (see Keely, 1982, and Bean, King, and Passel, 1985, for an overview of estimates). Almost all estimates of the aggregate economic and labor force effects of illegal migration had to be inferred from studies of all immigrants, making it difficult to test claims about sizable negative economic effects (see Bean, Telles and Lowell, 1987). But even though the evidence may have been confusing at times, public attitudes appeared more certain. If the residents of California provide any indication of national perceptions, then it seemed clear that a majority of the U.S. public perceived that illegal aliens were "a problem," that they took jobs away from some Americans, and that they eroded wages and working conditions of others (Muller and Espenshade, 1985). Although arguments were waged about what ways and to what degree undocumented migration in fact hurt or helped the economy, proposals to foster or maintain illegal immigration as a matter of public policy found few supporters. As a practical matter, however, it was not so clear how to reduce and contain illegal immigration.

Perceptions that the illegal immigrant flow was excessive were exacerbated by other developments during the 1970s. Cuban refugees continued to enter, followed by many Indochinese in 1975 with the fall of Saigon, and even more Indochinese with the 1978 influx of boat people. The United States accepted the lion's share of Indochinese refugees. The peak occurred when the United States agreed to take about 14,000 Indochinese per month in 1979. The March 1980 Refugee Act was meant to establish an orderly procedure for refugee flows. Soon after its passage, however, 125,000 Cubans arrived on our shores in the few months of the unplanned Mariel boat lift, joining a steady stream of Haitian boat people who had been landing uninvited in South Florida. And in the 1980s, Central Americans began to come to the United States and, like the Mariel Cubans, claimed asylum.

These refugee flows, combined with other developments, changed the national origin composition of immigrants from predominantly European to predominantly Latin and Asian. There were not only more immigrants overall, but increasingly more Third World immigrants. Illegal migration was also dominated by Hispanics from Caribbean and Latin American countries—even though it was not an exclusively Latin phenomenon. Refugees were coming mainly from Indochina and Cuba. All of these groups were different from the previous European immigrants and post–World War II refugees.

The Refugee Act of 1980 began to address some of the problems in this situation. It provided for a gradual decline in the number of refugee admissions through the setting of annual targets. From a level of 217,000 authorized admissions in 1981 to 66,000 in 1987, Congress and the Reagan administration restricted refugee resettlement. (For 1989, the authorized level is up to 94,000, mainly because of increased Soviet emigration made possible by *glasnost*.)

But illegal migration continued unchecked. Pressure began to build for legislation to control illegal flows. The chosen mechanisms included requirements that employers hire only citizens and residents authorized to work by the terms of their visas, as well as a set of graduated policy of fines and penalties for noncompliance that were intended to be stiff enough to make violation of the law more than a cost of doing business. Jobs at American wages, even at the low end of the wage distribution, were viewed by supporters of employer sanctions as the magnet that was attracting illegal immigrants. The assumption was that job opportunities could be reduced and illegal migration restricted to tolerable levels by prohibiting employers from hiring undocumented workers. And illegal aliens already in the country would slowly leave as layoffs and job changes meant they, too, faced difficulties in finding new jobs without proper documents.

Employer sanctions were opposed by groups who feared they would lead to discrimination, not only against persons of Latin and Asian ancestry but also against those who "looked foreign" or spoke English with a foreign accent. But supporters of employer sanctions finally prevailed, after a number of unsuccessful attempts to get legislation passed by Congress.

The Immigration Reform and Control Act of November 1986 was the result. It was aimed primarily at curbing illegal migration, but it also addressed the problem of illegal aliens already in the United States, the demands of agricultural employers for a transition process to meet perceived labor requirements, and the need for safeguards against employment discrimination. Legalization—the mechanism for dealing with illegal aliens already in the country—served to affirm the principle of legal immigration and to address the concern of protecting the civil rights of previously undocumented workers.

These objectives would not have been accomplished by other alternatives such as deportation. IRCA was, thus, a complex bill that mandated changes with potential impacts far beyond the issue of controlling U.S. borders.

Chapter 3 describes the major components of the IRCA package, chief among them being employer sanctions and legalization.

Notes

1. The right of petition is limited to adult citizens because, under U.S. citizenship law and practice, anyone born on U.S. territory (except the child of a foreign diplomat or his or her accredited staff) is a U.S. citizen. This is generally the case in countries that follow the common law tradition. To prevent women from coming to the United States solely to deliver a child and then have the citizen child petition for his or her parents, the immediate relatives petition is limited to adult citizens. A child born in the United States can claim citizenship regardless of whether the parents are here permanently or temporarily, legally or not.

2. Based on experience with attempts to clear backlogs in previous times, many analysts and officials believe that backlogs overstate the true numbers who would come forward if more visas were to become available. This list of names are not routinely purged, so that names remain in spite of death, loss of interest, or achievement of immigration goals in other ways.

3. The Washington, D.C. office of the United Nations High Commissioner for Refugees estimates that there are 13.5 million refugees worldwide. Special humanitarian interest as a criterion for settlement in the United States is not explicitly defined in the law. Few would deny that foreign or domestic policy interests and pressures lead in fact to declaring various groups to be of special humanitarian interest.

THE IMMIGRATION REFORM AND CONTROL ACT OF 1986

The passage of IRCA in October 1986 was preceded by a number of compromises among members of Congress. The main goal of the bill's sponsors was to enact employer sanctions to reduce illegal migration. A legalization program was required by advocates of ethnic and religious groups whose supporters in congress were strong enough to prohibit an employer sanctions bill unless it contained such a program. But legalization was still controversial. It survived a floor challenge in the House of Representatives to eliminate it by only seven votes just prior to the bill's passage.

Even an IRCA with the twin pillars of sanctions and legalization seemed unlikely to pass as late as September 1986. A third ingredient that led to the political viability of the bill was a series of provisions related to agricultural labor. A package was assembled under the leadership of Congressman Charles Schummer of New York. The Schummer amendments led to crucial support from southwestern and Californian delegations to move the bill for consideration in the House.

IRCA, as passed, underwent a number of metamorphoses. Congressional compromises resulted in a multifaceted bill with implications that exceeded control of illegal migration. IRCA is a major immigration law. But as this chapter's description of the law's primary provisions reveals, IRCA also affects employment, agricultural labor, civil rights, welfare, and federal reimbursement policies.

The congressional compromises and deal-making resulted in a law that mandated:

☐ *Employer requirements and sanctions*, making it illegal to hire undocumented workers;
☐ *Antidiscrimination safeguards* designed to prevent employment discrimination against foreign-looking and foreign-sounding citizens and legal aliens;

□ *A Legally Authorized Workers (LAWs)* program to regularize the status of aliens resident since 1982;
□ *A Special Agricultural Workers (SAWs)* legalization program to regularize the status of aliens who worked in agriculture up through 1986;
□ *A replenishment* program to admit additional immigrants for work in agriculture after 1990, if newly legalized immigrants move out of the agricultural sector for employment;
□ *A State Legalization Impact Assistance Grants (SLIAG)* program to pay states for additional costs of legalization under a cost reimbursement program of $4 billion over four years;
□ *A Systematic Alien Verification for Entitlements (SAVE)* program to check the eligibility of noncitizens for federally financed welfare; and
□ *Increased enforcement* with funds authorized for the U.S. Immigration and Naturalization Service (INS) and the U.S. Department of Labor (DOL).

Each of the major provisions of IRCA is reviewed briefly here to provide a context for chapter 4's discussion of the law's implementation.

EMPLOYER REQUIREMENTS, SANCTIONS AND ANTIDISCRIMINATION SAFEGUARDS

As of November 6, 1988, IRCA forbade employment of aliens unauthorized to work in the United States. After that date employers had to determine that all new hires were either (1) American citizens, (2) persons with a valid visa that permitted them to work, or (3) persons with work authorization from the Immigration and Naturalization Service while their immigration status was being decided (for example, applicants for asylum). Beginning on June 1, 1987, employers could receive citations if (1) they did not fill out a form (referred to as the I–9) for each new hire and (2) did not go back and fill out an I–9 form attesting to the eligibility of every hire after November 6, 1986.[1] Job applicants had to produce proof of identification and of eligibility to work. To accomplish this, the U.S. attorney general issued regulations designating documents that an employer had to inspect either to show citizenship (a passport or a combination of birth certificate and driver's license were the major ones permitted) or to prove that the applicant was a permanent resident alien or the holder of a temporary visa or other INS document permitting work in the United States.

Employers who knowingly hire a noncitizen unauthorized to work under immigration law are subject under IRCA to a civil penalty ranging from $250 to $2,000 per unauthorized alien for the first offense, $2,000 to 5,000 for the second offense, and up to a $3,000 to 10,000 fine per unauthorized alien for the third offense. Those who engage in "a pattern or practice" of knowingly hiring illegal aliens can be enjoined from doing so and, if they fail to stop, are subject to felony penalties of a $3,000 fine and/or six months imprisonment per violation. Employers who fail to inspect the documents of all new hires and who do not have the I-9 form filled out by these hires and available for government inspection are liable to penalties of $1,000 per employee.

Employment discrimination based on national origin was already illegal under U.S. Civil Rights law prior to the passage of IRCA. IRCA extended such protection to prohibit discrimination on the basis of citizenship status. It also extended employment discrimination protections to employers of 4 or more persons, a reduction from the 10 or more under the Civil Rights Act of 1964. Under IRCA an employer cannot refuse to hire noncitizens solely because they are not citizens, except in certain sensitive positions for which federal law or regulation requires citizenship. An employer can, however, favor a citizen over an alien if both applicants are otherwise equally qualified. Complaints about discrimination under the new procedures can be taken to the Office of Special Counsel on Employment Discrimination in the U.S. Department of Justice, established by IRCA specifically for that purpose.

To determine if a pattern of discrimination based on national origin is resulting from employer sanctions, the law mandates an annual report by the GAO to Congress for the first three years of the law's operation. The GAO must also include in the report assessments of whether the sanctions' provisions are being properly carried out, and of whether employers are bearing an unnecessary burden because of them (including the inspection of documents and paperwork). The law further requires the attorney general and the chairmen of the Civil Rights Commission and Equal Employment Opportunity Commission (EEOC) to appoint a task force to review the GAO annual reports and make legislative recommendations if discrimination has occurred. If after three years of operation Congress determines that sanctions have caused widespread discrimination, the law includes authorization for expedited procedures to end employer sanctions.

The penalties against employers for hiring undocumented aliens were not imposed until June 1987, six months after IRCA's passage. The reason for the delay was to allow time for public education. To achieve this goal, the INS undertook a massive education campaign, mailing over 10 million information packages to American employers and meeting with or telephoning 1.8 million employers in group meetings or individually. During the next 12 months (June 1987– May 1988) citations were issued with no sanction for first offenses; second or continued instances of illegal employment were subject to fines.

IRCA's employer requirements were intended by Congress to introduce a new set of hiring procedures that would become a normal and continuing practice by employers. The time allowed for an information campaign targeted at millions of U.S. employers and the phasing in of penalties were a deliberate effort to foster voluntary compliance. The presumptions were that voluntary compliance from the majority of employers would be effective over the long run in reducing illegal migration, and that by trying to educate and develop a clear set of procedures, the I–9 form process would be institutionalized as part of ordinary hiring practices by most employers.

Yet, Congress also intended employer sanctions to send a forceful message to both employers and illegal migrants, with penalties stiff enough to deter violations. The objective was "to stem the tide" of illegal migration immediately. The relative emphases and resources devoted to the different objectives of the legislation can lead to ambiguity in assessing the effectiveness of employer sanctions in the early years of IRCA. To evaluate IRCA's overall effectiveness in achieving the dual goals of quick and long-term deterrence of illegal migration requires criteria for balancing priorities related to each goal. The education campaign and phasing in of penalties may weaken the immediacy of "stemming the tide." To evaluate whether IRCA achieves its goals will depend to some extent on the priority given to the immediate versus the long-term effort to control illegal migration to the United States.

LEGALIZATION AND UNDOCUMENTED ALIENS
(THE LAWs PROGRAM)

To legalize undocumented aliens already residing in the United States, IRCA instituted two programs. The first of these was general legalization for those illegally resident in the country since January 1, 1982, and is referred to as the Legally Authorized Workers (LAWs) program. The second, which is discussed in the next section, was a special program for workers in the agricultural sector,[2] referred to as the Special Agricultural Workers (SAWs) program.

The LAWs program, or amnesty, as it was popularly but not entirely accurately referred to, was a one-time measure to permit persons who had been in an illegal status and residents since January 1, 1982, to apply for "permanent resident alien" status. The application period was for 12 months, beginning on May 5, 1987. Again, the 6-month gap between passage of the law and the initial application date was designated by the attorney general to allow time to gear up the program. LAWs applicants could register directly with the INS or through a "qualified designated entity" (QDE—state, local, and community agencies and voluntary organizations designated by the INS to receive applications and advise applicants). The QDEs, in turn, sent applications to the INS. Because of concern for privacy, the law mandates that information on any of the applications may be used only to judge the application. Data on the application are confidential, and the law limits use of them to making determinations for legalization. QDE files and records are similarly confidential, and the law bars access to them by the attorney general and the INS.

Approved applicants received temporary alien status. After 18 months, if the alien meets requirements showing English language and civics knowledge, and meets the usual health and criminal standards required of any immigrant, he or she may apply for and, if qualified, receive permanent resident alien status. Thus, the 18-month period serves as a trial to enable applicants to demonstrate language and civics knowledge, a commitment to stay in the United States, and the same general qualifications required by immigrants who enter in the normal way.

AGRICULTURAL WORKER PROVISIONS

To assure passage of the immigration control features of IRCA, a series of amendments were adopted to enable transition for the agricultural sector away from reliance on undocumented workers. The first such provision was the SAWs legalization program for special agricultural workers (SAWs). The registration period for the SAWs legalization ended in November 1988, about six months after the regular legalization program terminated.

The SAWs provision authorized temporary resident status for up to 350,000 agricultural workers in perishable crops who worked 90 person-days in each of the three years (1984–86) prior to the bill's enactment, with a change to permanent status allowed after one year. The bill also permitted any agricultural worker who worked on perishable crops for 90 person-days in the year ending May 1, 1986 (plus any applicants over the 350,000 limit of the previous program) to become a temporary resident and to obtain permanent status after two years.

The second provision for agricultural workers was a new temporary worker program in agriculture, the H–2A classification, providing expedited procedures for grower requests for foreign labor and review of denials.

The third provision established a four-year period (1990–93) under which "replenishment workers" can be admitted to temporary resident status if the secretaries of Agriculture and Labor certify that a shortage of agricultural workers exists (presumably because legalized seasonal agricultural workers leave agriculture to work in some other sector of the U.S. economy). The number of replenishment workers that can be admitted under this provision equals the need as determined by the secretaries of Labor and Agriculture minus the projected domestic supply for the year in question. Replenishment workers who perform 90 person days of seasonal agricultural services for three years will then become eligible for permanent resident status.

The final provision forbids INS officers to conduct searches in open fields for undocumented aliens without a warrant or the owner's consent.

The SAWs legalization program, which extended through November 1988, enrolled 1.3 million applicants, instigating accusations of widespread fraud. The number of claimants stretched credulity, given the absorptive capacity of seasonal agricultural work in the United States. In addition, anecdotes circulated of applicants demonstrating ludicrous ignorance of agriculture, saying that they picked baked beans and harvested strawberries in trees. Not surprisingly, forces are already marshaling to influence the decision of the secretaries of Labor and Agriculture on the need for replenishment workers in 1990.

STATE LEGALIZATION IMPACT ASSISTANCE GRANTS
(SLIAG)

Under the SLIAG program, IRCA authorized $1 billion per year for four years (beginning with FY 1988) to reimburse state governments for the costs of public assistance, health and educational services to the newly legalized. If applications from the states for reimbursement do not exhaust the appropriated funds at the end of the four years, unexpended SLIAG funds may be expended for legalization impacts through FY 1994.

SLIAG is administered by the U.S. Department of Health and Human Services. Funds are allotted to states by a formula that gives equal weight to the number of eligible legalized aliens and to the amount of SLIAG eligible costs in each state when each of these factors are expressed as a proportion whose denominator is the sum of each factor across all states. Some of the $1 billion a year will be used to pay federal costs as determined by the federal Office of Management and Budget which will apportion funds for federal and state costs.

The regulations specify that states may use the SLIAG funds for public assistance, medical assistance, education and administrative costs of providing services and complying with the regulations. The regulations go into some detail on eligible programs, limits on reimbursements per pupil and how funds are to be apportioned among public assistance, medical and health costs. Each state submits an application for the next fiscal year. The department reviews each application to evaluate the following criteria: whether activities proposed for reimbursement are allowable, the reasonableness of the estimates of participants; and the consistency of estimated cost per participant with past experience. Funds unexpended at the end of the program must be returned by the states.

SYSTEMATIC ALIEN VERIFICATION FOR ENTITLEMENTS
(SAVE) PROGRAM

Before IRCA, SAVE was an experimental program to assure that noncitizens were eligible for welfare benefits. IRCA requires all states to participate in SAVE in order to verify the immigration status of all aliens applying for certain federally funded public assistance programs. The costs of SAVE verification will be fully reimbursed by the federal government. For states that can document that SAVE verification is not cost effective, participation can be waived. The objective is to keep ineligible aliens from receiving federally funded public assistance programs. Applicants for public assistance whose immigrant status is unresolved are entitled by the IRCA legislation to a hearing.

INCREASED ENFORCEMENT

IRCA contained a sense-of-Congress provision that two essential elements for establishing immigration control were, first, increased border patrol, inspections, and other enforcement activities and, second, increased service activities to ensure prompt adjudication of petitions and applications. The emphasis of the law was on enforcement. Over $400 million, over and above other authorizations, was authorized with the goal of achieving a 50 percent increase in border patrol personnel in 1987 and 1988 over 1986 levels. To deter the employment of unauthorized aliens, IRCA also authorized budget increases for the Wage and Hour Division and the Office of Federal Contract Compliance Programs in the Department of Labor so that inspections of employer records could be carried out. Finally, the law established a $35 million immigration emergency fund to pay for border patrol and other enforcement activities or to reimburse state and local governments for assistance provided at the request of the attorney general in an immigrant emergency. To use the fund, the president must determine that an emergency situation exists and certify this to the Judiciary Committees in the House of Representatives and the Senate.

CONCLUSION

IRCA authorizes funds for education of employers and undocumented aliens, the groups most directly affected. The law also tried to anticipate negative effects and addressed them in its discrimination provisions, attention to agricultural labor, and required assessment of employer burden. The law further mandates numerous evaluations of its provisions by the president, implementing agencies, and the GAO. It provides, as well, for expedited procedures for

Congress to consider the effects of the law to allow "sunsetting" of some of IRCA's provisions if necessary. IRCA established a specific and different program to reach each of its various goals. Further, these programs were established in several different federal agencies, each with its own history, orientation, and mandate.

Legalization required a major INS effort to receive and review about 3 million applications in the regular legalization and special agricultural workers program. Employer sanctions required multiple efforts in several agencies. The INS had to mount a large public education effort aimed at employers, and also had to develop procedures and forms for review of employee eligibility for work. The INS and the Labor Department jointly conducted an enforcement effort, with Labor Department inspectors reviewing the I–9 forms. And the Justice Department set up the earlier-mentioned Office of Special Counsel to develop antidiscrimination procedures.

The agricultural labor issues, including the H–2A temporary visas and replenishment workers, will involve the departments of Labor, Agriculture, and Justice for many years. Public assistance issues required the INS to expand SAVE from a pilot program in a few states to all states, and the DHHS has had responsibility for running a $4 billion federal reimbursement program, of which $3 billion is supposed to go to the states by 1994. And the INS took on all of its additional mandates while increasing enforcement activities, especially along the border.

Thus, IRCA mandated large and complex new programs involving many government departments, billions of dollars, and tremendous public and private effort over many years. These programs potentially affect every worker in the country. Some of the programs require intense effort over a few years (for example, legalization, SLIAG, and replenishment); others continue indefinitely (for example, SAVE and review of employee eligibility for work). The claim with which this chapter began bears repeating. IRCA is not only an immigration law; it also makes notable changes in employment, agricultural labor, civil rights, and federal reimbursement policies and programs.

Notes

1. Congress postponed the beginning date for I–9s to be filled out from June 1, 1987, to September 5, 1987. Undocumented workers hired prior to November 6, 1986, were

"grandfathered" under the law (for example, they were permitted to continue working in that same job, and there was no sanction against employers).

2. IRCA also advanced the "registry" date from 1948 to 1972. This feature of immigration law permits anyone resident from before 1972 to apply for legal residence. The registry date provision has long been part of immigration law and should be distinguished from the one-time legalization program for those resident from 1982. Moving forward the registry date was not a controversial issue in Congressional debate. At the passage of IRCA in October 1986, a person would have to have been in the U.S. for almost 15 years to satisfy the 1972 date. Unlike the one-time legalization program, persons need fewer qualifications and there is no waiting period in a temporary status before immigrant status is granted. Therefore, there was an incentive for those who qualified to use the registry provision rather than undergo the legalization program. In 1988, almost 40,000 qualified under the updated registry provision, a larger number than anticipated.

Chapter Four

IMPLEMENTATION OF THE IMMIGRATION REFORM AND CONTROL ACT OF 1986

IRCA's programs and provisions are being implemented over a five-year period. To date, however, only one significant milestone has been reached: the closing of the formal application period for IRCA's two legalization programs.[1] The INS has reviewed and approved three out of four applications for the general legalization program (LAWs) and one-third of the applications for the special program for agricultural workers (SAWs). The second phase of legalization, processing applications for permanent residence by those now holding temporary residence visas, began in November 1988. Even though only one milestone has been reached, however, a wide range of IRCA-related activities has begun, as can be seen in table 4.1 (see also table A.1 in Appendix A).

Any final assessment of IRCA's implementation and effects must wait until at least the five-year implementation period is over. As input to that final assessment, ongoing monitoring of IRCA's progress serves a vital function of recording how the law is being put into practice, thereby providing a basis for assessment. This chapter reviews IRCA's progress through February 1989. The activities of the INS are discussed first, followed by those of the Department of Labor (DOL), state and local government agencies, the courts, and the more than 7 million employers, in that order.

In the summer of 1988, the Program for Research on Immigration Policy initiated a comprehensive comparative assessment of the implementation of IRCA's major programs across several sites, including Los Angeles, San José, El Paso, Houston, San Antonio, Miami, New York, and Chicago. Data collection for this study involves several waves of fieldwork over time and is still under way. Because it is too early to draw conclusions from this study, this chapter relies primarily on published data and other studies of IRCA implementations (see references).

Table 4.1 SUMMARY OF IRCA-RELATED ACTIVITIES (November 1986 to February 1989)

Legalization programs	
Number of applications filed under LAW Program	1.77 million
Number of applications filed under SAW Program	1.31 million
Employer education	
Number of handbooks distributed by INS	10.74 million
Number of employer contacts by INS	1.80 million
Enforcement of employer requirements	
Number of employers investigated	15,387
Number of employers cited or warned	3,683
Number of I-9 audits made by DOL	49,809
Enforcement of antidiscrimination provisions	
Number of discrimination charges received by Office of Special Counsel on Employment Discrimination	454
Agricultural special provisions	
Number of H–2A requests submitted to DOL	22,102
INS expenditures (FY 1988, in thousands)	1,024,356

Source: Appendix, table A.1.

IMMIGRATION AND NATURALIZATION SERVICE RESPONSIBILITIES

Before IRCA, the INS was responsible for naturalization and visa application services and for border and interior enforcement functions.[2] (Through interagency agreements, the INS and the U.S. Customs authorities share some duties at ports of entry. The INS also cooperates in many enforcement activities as a major border agency.) Under IRCA, the INS has become the federal agency with primary responsibility for implementing IRCA's two legalization programs, informing employers about the law's new requirements and enforcing these requirements. The large scale of these new programs, as well as stepped-up border enforcement, has profoundly affected INS operations. In the two years and a half since IRCA was passed, the number of INS personnel increased by more than 45 percent, to 17,000 employees; its overtime and holiday hours increased fourfold; and its budget (total obligations) increased by 42 percent, to more than $1 billion annually. Prior to 1986, revenues raised by the INS from inspections and naturalizations reverted to the federal general funds. However, since then, such fees accrue as revenues to the INS, and in 1988 they represented more than 20 percent of the INS budget.

The INS experienced a similarly large increase in its overall workload. In the 18 months from May 1987 to November 1988, it accepted more than 3 million applications for legalization, it reviewed and processed nearly half of them, and it sought to inform more than 7 million employers about their new responsibilities. At the same time the number of persons inspected, naturalization applications completed, and applications and petitions processed remained about the same as before passage of IRCA (table 4.2).

Finally, IRCA has thrust the INS into the public spotlight as never before. As one INS official put it, "We are now in the big leagues and everybody is looking at us to see whether or not we can actually perform" (Norton, 1988).

Legalization Programs

IRCA's two legalization programs,[3] as noted, were legislated as one-time temporary programs that would be terminated after permanent residence was granted to the last eligible applicants in 1991. With no previous experience in operating such programs, the INS had six months to plan, design, and start operating the LAWs application process beginning on May 5, 1987, and the SAWs application process beginning on June 1, 1987.

Two early major decisions helped shape the implementation of the legalization programs. The first involved a decision not to request federal funds to operate the programs with tax revenues, but to fully self-fund the programs with application fees. Applicants for legalization were charged a fee of $185 per adult and $50 per minor child, with a maximum of $420 per family.[4]

The second decision was one to manage and administer the legalization programs through the existing decentralized network of 4 regions and 33 domestic INS districts (North and Portz, 1988), with the central office setting general guidelines, directives, and programmatic goals. Hence, within those parameters, regional commissioners and district directors had flexibility and tailored their legalization activities—as well as other activities related to IRCA—to circumstances in the field.

For operations, however, the INS chose facilities that were physically separate from its enforcement-related activities and other regular service activities. It opened 109 new offices throughout the country to handle up to an estimated 3.9 million applications for the two legalization programs (Hoefer, 1988a).[5]

As already noted, applications also could be filed with a network of 980 sites sponsored by some 200 voluntary agencies and com-

Table 4.2 INS BUDGET, PERSONNEL, AND WORKLOAD, FY 1985–90

Budget and Selected Workload Indicators	1985 Actual	1986 Actual	1987 Actual	1988 Actual	1989 Estimate	1990 Budget
Budget ($ millions)						
Total direct program	580	574	651	808	832	866
Enforcement	340	361	391	480	541	583
Reimbursable program[a]	19	20	193	217	207	204
Total obligations	599	594	844	1,024	1,039	1,071
Personnel						
Full-time equivalent employment[b]	11,268	11,656	12,413	14,773	16,999	16,032
Full-time overtime and holiday hours	3,569	1,473	3,901	5,217	5,119	5,114
Selected workload indicators (thousands)						
Total persons inspected	307,657	328,042	297,020	341,078	350,000	350,000
Naturalization applications completed	524	434	407	404	430	460
Other applications and petitions completed by adjudication and naturalization	2,185	1,357	2,140	2,287	3,110	3,450
Border patrol						
Apprehensions	1,262	1,693	1,158	969	980	1,110
Smuggled aliens apprehended	96	115	62	50	51	57
Investigations						
Deportable aliens apprehended[c]	71	60	31	37	83	83

Sources: Presidential budgets, appendices to the budget for FY 1987, FY 1988, FY 1989 and FY 1990.
a. Revenues from fees funding INS operations.
b. Includes direct and reimbursable positions.
c. Includes both casework and noncasework activities.

munity organizations (qualified designated entities [QDEs]), which signed an agreement with INS to participate in the legalization program. In setting up QDEs, Congress was responding to concerns that undocumented aliens would be reluctant to apply for legalization because they did not trust the INS. Authority to review and approve applications remained with the INS, however.

Persons eligible for the SAWs program living abroad at the beginning of the amnesty period were permitted a third application route. They could apply at U.S. consulates abroad or at border entry stations in Calexico, Otay Mesa in California, and Laredo in Texas.[6] These applicants paid the full fee but needed only to submit a partial application to receive authorization to enter and work in the United States for 90 days.

By the time the amnesty application period ended—on May 4, 1988, for the legalization program and November 30, 1988, for the SAWs program—more than 1.7 million and 1.3 million applications, respectively, had been submitted.[7] Nearly half of these were filed in the last third of the respective application periods. About 71 percent of the applications were filed directly by the client with the INS, 21 percent through QDEs, and the remaining 8 percent through a lawyer.[8]

Review of applications for legalization is centralized at four processing centers, one at each of the four INS regions. By February 1989, these processing centers had reviewed 1.7 million applications (55 percent of all applications submitted).

Virtually all applications that have been reviewed by the INS for LAWs eligibility have been approved with applicants granted temporary residence for 18 months.[9] At the end of that time, they have one year to apply for permanent residence. One in four applications (about 450,000) have not yet been reviewed.

In the SAWs program, 94 percent of applications reviewed to date have been approved and the applicants granted temporary residence. Of those approved, up to 350,000 will "automatically"[10] become permanent residents in December 1989 and the balance in December 1990.[11] Nearly three out of four SAWs applications (about 935,000) had yet to be reviewed as of February 1989.

In November 1988, the INS began to accept applications for permanent residence from temporary residents granted legalization under the LAWs program. As of January 1989, fewer than one in six of those eligible to apply for permanent residence has applied, once again raising concerns that temporary residents were not adequately informed of the program requirements and, thus, are not fully aware that they must newly apply for permanent residence. To date, nearly all applications for permanent residence that have been reviewed (about 23,000) have been approved.

To date, no systematic comprehensive study of the implementation of the legalization programs has been completed.[12] But two studies (Meissner and Papademetriou, 1988; North and Portz, 1988) suggest that the programs have evolved over time, under pressure from the courts and advocacy groups, toward a liberalization of the rules of eligibility. Writing in February 1988, Meissner and Papademetriou found that "since the application began, INS has made important adjustments, modifications and clarifications to the regulations."

The INS also made administrative changes to ease undocumented workers' access to temporary residence. Concerns were expressed in the early part of 1988, for example, about the "lag" in the applications for the LAWs and the SAWs programs. Consequently, the INS agreed to pay a recruiter fee[13] for each applicant directed to an INS legalization office and to allow 60 days after the May 4, 1988, deadline for applicants to provide the necessary documentation and medical information to support their applications. The INS also began to accept employer affidavits instead of pay stubs or other supporting evidence of eligibility for legalization, although this practice reportedly varied over time and across INS districts.

About 140,000 persons applied for the SAWs program through the INS offices opened in Mexico for this purpose. About 103,000 of these applicants (8 percent of all SAWs applicants) were allowed to enter the country. Of these entrants, 70 percent eventually followed up by bringing their full documentation to schedule interviews with the INS.[14]

Observers have noted other changes in the direction of easing the access of undocumented workers to temporary residence. These include development over time of improved relationships and cooperation between the INS, QDEs, and other agencies serving immigrants in many local areas. In brief, the INS demonstrated that it could mobilize staff quickly to implement a large-scale new function, and that it could become more open, exhibiting considerable regulatory and administrative flexibility throughout the legalization application process.

However, the same observers have noted a number of problems in the operation of the legalization programs. Perhaps the most important criticisms have been levied at the initial regulations and formal nationwide public information effort. Regarding the first, many of the early comments and testimonies before Congress were directed at the INS's "rigid" interpretation of the law and of congressional intent as reflected in its final INS regulations for the legalization programs. These criticisms were directed at issues such as the definition of "known to government"; the requirement that aliens be physically present in the U.S. after the November 6, 1986, enactment date; standards for granting waivers; and the matter of whether applicants would be required to relinquish original documents. Some of these issues receded in importance over time because changes in INS regulations or because they seemed, in the end, not to cause problems. Others became the object of litigations (see "The Courts" later in this chapter).

Also, the initial nationwide public information effort seems to have been inadequate, especially for non-Spanish-speaking undocumented aliens, leaving much of the task for information and outreach to INS field staff, churches, community organization, and the media (Meissner and Papademetriou, 1988). A new national advertising effort was started in January 1988 to improve the targeting of ethnic groups in various parts of the country.[15]

Other implementation problems have been identified, including delays in finalizing and publishing regulations on legalization;[16] changes and clarifications in the law that were not adequately communicated to community groups, and immigrants and were not uniformly heeded by the various INS offices (Meissner and Papademetriou, 1988; North and Portz, 1988); lack of clarity in promulgated regulations (North and Portz, 1988); and, reportedly, lack of uniformity in regulations and documentation requirements over time and among INS regions, districts, and local offices.[17] Finally, concerns have been raised about inadequate attention given to fraud, particularly in the SAWs program.[18]

Some of these issues may represent operating problems that were peculiar to the early period of the programs, and most have yet to be fully documented. Thus, it remains to be assessed whether these problems represented operational frictions that had no major effects or whether they will prove to have significantly affected the outcome of IRCA's legalization programs.

As the legalization programs are moving into their second phase, two ongoing issues are raising particular concern. One is the backlog of some 1.3 million legalization applications for temporary residence that remained to be reviewed and adjudicated by INS regional centers. During the time these applications are being processed, applicants are be uncertain about their status, while employers are uncertain about whether they are authorized to work. The second concern is the slow start of the second phase of the legalization program, with only one in six of those eligible to apply for permanent residence having done so as of early 1989. Mirroring developments that occurred during the temporary residence application phase, there are calls for a more aggressive outreach and information campaign, as well as questions about the adequacy of staffing resources devoted to this effort.

Employer Education and Requirements

The INS adhered closely to the phased implementation of the employer requirements and eventual sanctions, as intended by Congress. As noted earlier in this report, the first six months, beginning in December 1986, were to be a public education period, followed by a 12-month period during which citations would be issued for first-time violations. Thus, in the early stages of IRCA's implementation (lasting through June 1988), the INS declared itself to be in an "educational mode," approaching this new function in a cooperative spirit (Schroeder, 1988) and seeking voluntary compliance rather than writing citations (GAO, 1987d).[19]

In pursuing its education task, the INS launched a $2.5 million national media campaign to explain what the new law required from employers with regard to certification of all new hires; at the same time, less attention was paid to the law's antidiscrimination provisions. The INS also distributed some 7 million handbooks to employers in June, July, and August of 1987, outlining what was expected of them and their liabilities should they fail to comply (GAO, 1988e). At the urging of advocacy groups, the INS also asked and Congress eventually agreed to delay for three months (from June 1, 1987, to September 1, 1987) the requirement that the employer complete the I–9 form used to certify that an employee is authorized to work in this country.[20] Finally, the INS allocated 50 percent of its investigative time and assigned its border patrol agents to contact a target of 1 million employers by telephone or in person by June 1, 1988.[21]

The INS is treating the education of employers regarding their responsibilities under IRCA as an ongoing mandate. Employer education was not entirely phased out after June 1, 1988, although resources allocated to employer information were reduced to 25 percent (from 50 percent) of time spent on investigative activities with a new target of contacting 500,000 additional employers by June 1989 (GAO, 1988e). At the same time, a new office of Employer and Labor Relations headed by an assistant commissioner, was created to "help employers, labor and management groups, civic and community organizations, and others affected by the Act understand and abide by the law" (Schroeder, 1988). This office also is responsible for developing and overseeing a new service to help employers find authorized workers for jobs formerly held by unauthorized aliens. This Legally Authorized Worker Program, started in late 1986, is intended to provide employers with information on sources of legal labor in all 50 states.

In reality, INS efforts to enforce IRCA's prohibition against hiring undocumented workers and I–9 procedures for all new employees began before the major thrust of the education effort ended. The first citation was issued in August 1987, and the first "intent to fine" citation for employing undocumented aliens was issued in October of that year. From June 1987 to May 1988, as allowed by the law, the INS restricted its enforcement efforts for first offenders to citations only. On June 1, 1988, it began full enforcement of the employer sanctions for first offenses, and stopped issuing citations to all employers, with the exception of agricultural growers.[22] However, consistent with INS continuing informational efforts, a warning notice can still be issued (instead of a notice of an "intent to fine") for first violations under specified circumstances.[23]

For FY 1988, the INS had established a goal of 20,000 inspections. It actually completed about 12,000 in that time. The number of employer inspections has not increased in FY 1989; in the first five months of FY 1989, about 5,000 employers have been inspected—the same number as in FY 1988.

Inspections may be initiated in one of two ways: (1) as a result of a lead based on local information (including complaints, Federal Bureau of Investigation [FBI] tips, knowledge, suspicion that certain firms hire undocumented workers, or records of past violations); or (2) through a random selection of firms done centrally at INS headquarters in Washington, D.C. Half of the firms selected are to be from economic sectors that used to employ significant numbers of unauthorized aliens (as determined by local district management) and half are from all other employers (GAO, 1988e). As of February 1989, 75 percent of inspections were based on leads and 25 percent were random. The intent is to eventually have 60 percent of resources devoted to the first type of inspections and 40 percent to the second.

Border Patrol and Other Enforcement Activities

While INS management attention and available resources were focused primarily on its major new, and most visible, responsibilities, other traditional INS enforcement activities, including border and interior enforcement, declined. In the interior, the number of undocumented deportable aliens apprehended in FY 1987 and FY 1988 declined by nearly 50 percent relative to the pre-IRCA years, as shown in table 4.2.[24] The INS expects interior apprehensions, however, to revert to their pre-IRCA levels in FY 1989 and FY 1990 (U.S. Office of Management and Budget, 1989).

At the border and as part of IRCA's enhanced enforcement strategy, Congress authorized a 50 percent increase in the 3,600 personnel in the border patrol for FY 1987 and FY 1988. As of the end of FY 1988 there were 4,699 staff in the border patrol, with about 3,700 agents actually deployed at the border and other field offices throughout the country.[25] By February 1989, 4,919 border patrol personnel totaled still short of the originally intended strength of the force. Two factors seem to have delayed the buildup of the border patrol force. The first factor has been a lag in actual appropriations of funds for INS enforcement: a sizable (33 percent) increase in the INS enforcement budget did not occur until FY 1988 (see table 4.2). And the second factor has been difficulties encountered in recruiting and expanding training staff and facilities.

As the size of the border patrol has increased, so has its IRCA-related and other responsibilities. Although unanticipated by Congress, the border patrol added to its responsibilities those of educating employers about their new IRCA-related requirements and enforcing these requirements. An indicator of the extent of the border patrol's employer sanctions enforcement effort is suggested by the fact that one out of three citations and notices of "intent to fine" was issued by border patrol agents nationwide, and about one out of two of these was in the southern and western INS regions.

Also starting in 1986, as IRCA was being implemented, interdiction of drug traffic across U.S. land borders became a prime focus of the border patrol. In the Tucson area, for instance, 250 agents were allocated to work with the Drug Enforcement Agency on Operation Alliance. This new emphasis was accompanied by an increase in the border patrol involvement in intelligence gathering on drug traffickers (as well as large alien smuggling operations).[26] Finally, the border patrol also had to expand the number of staff assigned to guard refugee camps—including the Oakdale camp outside of Atlanta, which housed aliens from the Mariel boatlift still being held for deportation proceedings—as well as to allocate more resources to identify, prosecute, and deport criminal aliens.

As a result, resources allocated by the border patrol to prevent crossings of the border by illegal immigrants have not been increased relative to the fiscal years preceding IRCA's legislation (as shown in table 4.3). Compared to FY 1986, total line-watch hours (direct patrolling) at the border in FY 1987 increased slightly during the first two quarters and started decreasing in the third quarter. By FY 1988, line-watch hours had decreased by 14 percent, although they were still slightly higher than in the pre-IRCA years. In addition, the share of actual line-watch hours devoted to interdiction of illegal immigration proper declined as more hours were being devoted to drug interdiction. Available data however, do not permit a measure of the extent of this shift.

Interdiction by immigration border patrol of illegal activities away from the immediate border—at airports, bus stations, and highway checkpoints—also has declined, as indicated by a 20 percent relative decrease in the number of "other than line-watch" apprehensions (see table 4.3).

In summary, INS's IRCA enforcement activities over the past two years has been directed primarily at informing employers about the new requirements affecting them. Enforcement through employer inspections is being maintained at its FY 1988 level, although, as we note later, reliance on fines instead of warning citations has increased significantly. Neither at the border nor at interior locations has there yet been an increase in enforcement activities focusing on illegal immigration.

Table 4.3 BORDER PATROL RESOURCE ALLOCATION AND ACTIVITY
INDICATORS

Indicators	Fiscal Year				
	1985	1986	1987	1988	1989
Number of border patrol staff	3,473	3,687	3,643	4,669	4,919[a]
Line-watch hours (thousands)	1,912	2,401	2,546	2,069	NA
Line-watch apprehensions (thousands)	666	946	751	615	NA
Percentage of total citations/ warnings issued by border patrol	—	—	—	35	NA
Percentage of total border patrol apprehensions not made at border	43	41	33	34	NA

Source: U.S. Immigration and Naturalization Service.
Notes: NA, not available; a dash (—), not applicable.
a. As of February 1989.

DEPARTMENT OF LABOR

The major IRCA-related activities participated in by the Department Labor are inspections of employers to verify compliance with IRCA's requirements and implementation of the H–2A program for agricultural employers.

Inspections

The INS shares the responsibility of inspecting employers' I–9 forms with the DOL, which added this task to the regular responsibilities of its Wage and Hour Division (WHD), which enforces a wide range of laws establishing standards for wages and working conditions, and its Office of Federal Contract Compliance Programs (OFCCP), whose primary responsibility is to enforce laws prohibiting discrimination on the basis of race, color, religion, gender, or national origin (GAO, 1988e).

The DOL began to inspect employers' I–9 forms in addition to its other duties on September 1, 1987. It planned to inspect 60,000 employers in FY 1988 (GAO, 1987d), but completed only slightly more than half that number (36,600). In the first part of FY 1989, inspections have been maintained at the same level as in FY 1988 (about 3,000 a month). To date, nearly 50,000 inspections of I–9 forms have been completed, more than 80 percent of which were made by the WHD. The DOL must provide employers with a three-day notice of forthcoming I–9 inspections, as must the INS. Results of DOL inspections are then forwarded to the INS, indicating apparent compliance or noncompliance with I–9 requirements, apparent unfair employment practices, and possible employment of unauthorized workers. A narrative may (but does not always) accompany the report, and the INS's decision to further investigate relies heavily on that narrative.[27]

To carry out its added responsibilities, the DOL's budget for FY 1988 was increased by $3.8 million and 68 positions. The budget for FY 1989 has been increased further, to $5 million and 91 positions (GAO, 1988e).

The H–2A Program

As of June 1987, the DOL also implemented the H–2A Temporary Agricultural Workers Program. This program, similar to the H–2 program that preceded it, allows individual agricultural employers wider use of temporary foreign workers when labor shortages can be demonstrated and certified by the DOL. IRCA streamlined this program by requiring DOL determinations to be made within set time periods.

Expectations were that this program would grow tenfold, to reach 200,000 workers by 1989 (Bruening, 1988; GAO, 1988c). In its first year of operation (July 1987 to June 30, 1988), however, the volume handled by the H–2A program did not differ from that handled by its predecessor H–2 program. About 20,000 temporary workers were authorized for admission, at the request of about 1,700 employers (DOL, 1988), roughly the same amount as in recent years (GAO, 1988c). Four out of five applications were approved, most of which were made by East Coast and mid-Atlantic agricultural growers. According to the DOL, government agencies conducted an educational campaign to publicize the program in late 1987 and early 1988. The DOL attributes low utilization of the program to an adequate supply of labor, in part due to lower demand for labor because of the drought. Western employers, in particular, had minimal demand for H–2A workers.[28] The availability of workers because of the SAWs program may also have contributed to the adequacy of the labor supply. The DOL anticipates that the program will grow in 1989 (DOL, 1988).

STATE AND LOCAL GOVERNMENTS

Under IRCA's State Legalization Impact Assistance Grants (SLIAG), state and local governments can be compensated for the increased costs of providing services to the newly legalized population. One billion dollars in federal funds for each of four years (beginning in FY 1988) were appropriated for this purpose. IRCA also mandated states' participation in the INS's Systematic Alien Verification for Entitlements (SAVE) system starting in October 1988.[29] Other than that, the legislation did not anticipate any specific implementation responsibilities or roles for state and local governments. Nevertheless, IRCA offers ample opportunities for states and localities to support, contribute to, or, by turn, make more difficult the implementation of IRCA's many provisions. These opportunities include antidiscrimination provisions and any requirements that states and localities impose on employers.

Prior to IRCA, 11 states—including the high-immigration states of California and Florida—had passed legislation prohibiting the hiring of undocumented aliens, although none of these states aggressively enforced these laws (Espenshade et al., 1988).[30] Any implementation study of IRCA must ask whether and to what extent IRCA may be (1) spurring states to expand existing activities or to implement new initiatives regarding immigrants and/or (2) heightening states' interests and stakes in national immigration and immigrant policies.

No systematic assessment of these questions has yet been completed. However, there are indications of increased state activity in several areas related to IRCA's implementation:

□ Legalization: Several states have provided funding to support outreach to undocumented aliens, eligible for legalization.

□ Worker Certification: Twenty-nine states had indicated (as of July 1987) that their employment agencies already provided or would provide the job applicants they refer to the INS with certification of employment eligibility.[31]

□ Antidiscrimination: In 1987, New York State established an Inter-Agency Task Force on Immigration Affairs (1988) to (1) develop appropriate safeguards to discourage IRCA-related discrimination and (2) ensure that, to the maximum extent possible, undocumented illegal aliens in New York State would avail themselves of the opportunity to obtain temporary legal status. Illinois also established a Commission on Human Rights to help collect information on IRCA discrimination and to assist individuals.

□ Enforcement: Several localities—mostly in the South and West, including Los Angeles—have passed or are considering local ordinances prohibiting employers from picking up day labor—mostly undocumented aliens—at street corners or parking lots and/or are conducting these activities at off-street sites.

THE COURTS

When a new law is implemented, its legislated policies and the "intent of Congress" must be translated into a set of operational regulations developed by the federal executive agencies. The process involves a period for public comment on the drafted regulations, during which time interested parties can challenge the federal agencies' implicit interpretations of the legislation. Once these rules and regulations have been finalized and published in the Federal Register by the agencies, they become the operating guidelines for implementation of the law and can be challenged in the courts.

In the past, court challenges have frequently been used to interpret the law, although typically not so early in the implementation of a new program as has been the case with IRCA. One reason for this unusual pattern is the temporary nature of the legalization programs and the limited window for their application. Another reason is IRCA's restriction on judicial review of denial of applications. The statute prohibits judicial review of individual case denials effectively curtailing use of the usual method of after-the-fact review of regulations, policies, and laws pertaining to a particular benefit program.

Court challenges to INS regulations and policies were filed almost as soon as the final regulations for the amnesty programs were issued. To date, more than 25 lawsuits have been filed in various federal district courts around the country. Most are class-action lawsuits (on behalf of undocumented aliens in the class) seeking liberalization of the policies and regulations guiding eligibility for the two legalization programs. Challenges over INS interpretations or policies have included the following:

☐ The definition that "known to the government" means known to the INS exclusively, rather than including other government agencies such as the Social Security Administration or the Internal Revenue Service;

☐ The policy of deporting and of preventing applications of persons eligible for legalization because they are in exclusion proceedings;

☐ The requirement that legalization-eligible aliens who left the United States after May 1, 1987, for a "brief, casual, and innocent" absence must have obtained advance permission for such absences for their eligibility to have been preserved;

☐ The denial of SAW status to aliens who were apprehended or issued orders to "show cause" after November 6, 1988 but who did not apply for SAW status within the first 30 days of the application period;

☐ The denial of eligibility to those who used a fraudulently obtained visa or other document to reenter the United States after January 1, 1982, to resume an unlawful residence;

☐ The denial of eligibility to undocumented aliens here prior to 1982 who left the country for a short absence and reentered with a non-immigrant visa;

☐ The use of past rather than future work ability as the test of likelihood of becoming a public charge;

☐ The use of welfare receipt by one household member to deny eligibility based on the public-charge clause of another household member;

☐ The need for employer verification of days worked and burden of proof of eligibility for the SAWs program;

☐ The U.S. Department of Agriculture (USDA) definition of SAW, eligible crops and the exclusion of sugar cane, cotton, and sod as perishable crops.

Most of the lawsuits are national in scope, but a few are challenging regional INS practices. One case (*Haitian Refugee Center v. Nelson*) applies only to Florida, Georgia, and Alabama, challenging a number of INS practices and policies, including the imposition of an "improper" burden of proof on applicants regarding the SAWs program in that region. Another (*Hernandez v. Meese*) applies only to the INS western region, challenging the lack of procedures or standards for obtaining waivers of the rule that single absences in excess of 45 days and aggregate absences in excess of 180 days after January 1, 1982, break the period of continuous residence. Yet another (*Loe v. Thornburgh*) applies to the eastern region, challenging INS's alleged failure to give proper weight to affidavits and to allow hearings with live testimony. And finally, *International Moulders' and Allied Workers' Local Union No. 164 v. Nelson* is being tried in San Francisco, challenging the INS's right to search businesses without a search warrant.

To date, only one lawsuit has been brought on behalf of a party other than undocumented aliens. In this case, the AFL-CIO is challenging the DOL's H–2A adverse-effect wage rate formula, claiming that it does not protect U.S. farmworkers.

Many of these lawsuits are still being litigated or are being appealed, but a pattern has emerged: courts have overruled the administration's positions and generally have granted the relief sought. Advocates indicate, however, that the INS is slow in implementing the court-ordered remedies.

EMPLOYERS

IRCA affects more than 7 million employers and millions of newly hired people every year. Employers are required to maintain on file for a three-year period the INS I–9 forms attesting that they have inspected specified work eligibility and identification documents submitted by the employee. In addition, employers with four or more employees are prohibited from intentionally discriminating against anyone—in recruiting or referral for a fee, in hiring, or in discharging employees—on the basis of country of origin or citizenship.[32] Failure to meet these requirements subjects employers to civil and criminal penalties.

Congress explicitly allowed for an 18-month transition period ending June 1988, during which time employers were to be informed of their new responsibilities and could begin to fulfill the new requirements without threat of sanctions for first-time violations. Seasonal agricultural employers were given an additional six months (to December 1988) without threat of sanctions for first-time violations.

Voluntary Compliance

Congress expected that employers would generally comply voluntarily after being informed about the law and understanding its multiple provisions.[33] The majority of employers who are aware of the IRCA provisions are in at least partial compliance. Employer surveys conducted during 1988 indicate that from 78 percent to 87 percent of employers were aware of the employer sanctions provisions under IRCA.[34] Of these, a majority (85 percent or more) knew they had to fill out the I–9 forms. However, a smaller percentage understood the full extent of the I–9 documentation requirements or knew about all of the major provisions of the law, including IRCA's antidiscrimination provisions. The GAO (1988e) estimated that, in spring 1988, 20 percent or more of employers did not clearly understand the circumstances allowing hiring preference to be given to a U.S. citizen over an alien.

As of late 1987, 50 percent of employers surveyed who knew about the I–9 procedural requirements, and had hired at least one employee between November 1986 and October 1987, had fully had complied with the requirements voluntarily (GAO, 1988e). Another 12 percent complied partially. Taking into account those who did not know about IRCA's requirements, about one in every two employers was fully or partially complying by late 1987.[35]

The DOL's I–9 audits indicate a similar rate of voluntary compliance: a 57 percent apparent full or partial compliance for the firms it inspected during FY 1988 and a 62 percent full or partial compliance for the first part of FY 1989. Finally, the INS reported an overall 68 percent compliance in the 16,500 investigations it had made through February 1989. As expected, compliance was higher (93 percent) among employers investigated randomly than among employers investigated as a result of complaints (60 percent). The INS's apparent practice of labeling compliance based on an employer's "willingness to comply" rather than actual compliance explains its reported higher rates, particularly for its inspections of firms selected randomly.

Knowledge of and compliance with IRCA's provisions seems to be correlated with firm size and with INS contacts and visits with the employer. More of the larger firms knew about IRCA requirements, so, in consequence, more of them complied. And compliance is as high as 80 percent for employers who were visited by INS either before or after IRCA's enactment (GAO, 1988e).[36]

Noncompliance seems to be correlated with administrative problems (for example, inadequate supply of I–9s or misunderstanding of I–9 verification requirements), with employers' perceptions of the sanction threat (for example, the employer did not believe he or she could be sanctioned or did not expect an INS visit), and with how difficult it was for the employer to locate authorized workers.

Enforcement

As of January 1989, about 70,000 employers had been investigated by the INS or audited by DOL inspectors to verify compliance with the I–9 requirements and the prohibition against hiring illegal workers. The INS issued a total of 3,683 citations or warnings. It also issued 1,387 intents to fine, for a total amount of about $6 million.

The INS southern region has been much more heavily involved in issuing notices of "intent to fine" than have the other three INS regions. Nearly half the total notices of intent to fine were issued in the southern INS region;[37] and notices of intent to fine in the southern region were running at about 50 percent of total citations and warnings issued, compared to 12 percent to 18 percent in the other three INS regions. Similar differences are apparent among INS districts and sectors, as well as regions, suggesting that there may be significant variations in enforcement strategies.

To date, 610 (44 percent) of the notices of intent to fine issued, amounting to $1 million, are final orders issued after negotiating and/or settlements by a district director or administrative hearing officer. The INS has collected $560,000. One in five employers receiving such a notice has requested a hearing. All but four of these hearings are pending.

Violation of the prohibition against hiring illegal aliens is the primary reason for notices of intent to fine, accounting for three out of five notices. The balance were for "paperwork violations." So far, most notices (three out of four as of October 1988) have gone to employers in the service sector. Investigations of firms in the service and construction sectors result in twice as high a proportion of notices of intent to fine as in the heavy or light industry sectors. Since enforcement in the agricultural sector did not become effective until December 1988, this pattern may well change.

As expected, INS notices of intent to fine increased significantly beginning in June 1988, when the INS was permitted to sanction employers (in all sectors other than agriculture) for first-time violations. In the eight-month period following June 1, 1988, 1,259 intents to fine were issued, compared with about 102 in the first 18 months after passage of IRCA. The proportion of total notices/ warnings that were notices of intent to fine increased from 17 percent in FY 1988 to 54 percent in the first few months of FY 1989. The value of the average intended fine decreased slightly, however, from about $5,000 to $4,300 per employer.

Effectiveness of the enforcement of IRCA's prohibition to hire undocumented workers may eventually be affected by the potentially widespread use of counterfeit documents. In a limited survey by the GAO of employed unauthorized aliens hired between September 1987 and October 1988, 39 percent had provided or were suspected of using counterfeit documents, primarily fake Social Security or alien registration cards (GAO, 1988e). Similarly, 41 percent of the respondents to a 1987–88 survey of undocumented aliens on street corners in San Diego acknowledged they had either purchased fraudulent documents or borrowed documents belonging to a friend or relative to gain employment (Cornelius, 1988).

In addition, a recent study by the GAO (1988d) concluded that "under IRCA, too many documents can be used for employment eligibility purposes to realistically expect employers to control unauthorized employment." It also concluded that the documents used for the Social Security number application and those used for employment authorization are vulnerable to fraud. To date, education of employers on document review and acceptance has been minimal, and the GAO questions the feasibility of educating employers on the large number of acceptable documents. GAO, therefore, recommends reducing the number of documents that can be used for employment authorization and making the Social Security card (after improving its issuance process) the only authorizing document.[38]

CONCLUSIONS

Since it was signed into law on November 6, 1986, IRCA has required a large-scale effort involving the simultaneous implementation of several complex programs, the mobilization of a large amount of resources, and the active involvement of several federal, state, and local agencies, nearly 7 million employers, and millions of individuals, both immigrants and native born.

It is not too early to assert that the INS, the leading implementing agency, has been transformed by it. Its budget and staff have increased by nearly 50 percent in less than two years. Both its enforcement and service functions have been expanded in areas where it had no previous experience. In the process, the INS has been subjected to public scrutiny as never before.

With no previous experience in running a legalization program, the INS designed, set up facilities, and hired and trained staff to eventually accept more than 3 million applications for legalization, all in less than two years. Begun in an atmosphere of mutual suspicion between the INS and advocates of immigrants, the legalization program has evolved over time toward a liberalization of its rules of eligibility and its administration. Advocacy groups played a major role in this process, both through political pressure and the use of litigation to force changes in regulations. As mentioned earlier, the latter began earlier than is typical in new entitlement programs because of the temporary nature of the program and because of IRCA's statutory limit on "after-the-fact" judicial review of individual legalization decisions.

To date, ambivalence has characterized reviews by observers of and participants in the legalization programs. Several criticisms of the programs' implementation have been levied along with praise for the programs' overall numerical success and the quality of the INS response. Of the criticisms, three stand out. The first concerns the apparent inadequacy of formal outreach and public information (particularly during the early part of the legalization program). The second concerns the apparent lack of uniformity in the program's administration and regulations across the INS's 4 regions and 33 domestic districts. In both cases, it remains to be seen whether these perceived inadequacies had major effects on the participation of eligible immigrants in the legalization programs.

The third criticism concerns the large number (some 1.3 million) of applications for temporary residence that have yet to be processed (as of February 1989). As stated earlier, while decisions are pending, applicants remain uncertain of their status and employers remain uncertain about whether these applicants are authorized to work or not.

The implementation of IRCA's employer requirements and sanctions were phased in over time. As of early 1989, the INS continued to be more in an "education" mode, seeking voluntary compliance, than in an "enforcement" mode. As of late 1987, one out of two employers were fully or partially complying. Of those who did not comply, nearly half were not fully aware of IRCA's requirements and eventual sanctions for noncompliance. Additional informational activities are being targeted to these employers. To encourage compliance, the INS also has begun to use the threat of sanctions more frequently. But the INS has yet to increase its frequency of inspections and the average size of its fine. There is evidence of variations in enforcement among regions and districts. Thus, the intent of Congress that "the immigration laws of the U.S. should be enforced vigorously and uniformly" remains to be fully carried out.

While INS management attention and available resources have been focused primarily on its new legalization and employer-related responsibilities, its border and interior enforcement directed to illegal immigrants have declined and are now lower than they were in the years immediately preceding IRCA's enactment. This is attributable in part to delays in increasing the number of staff assigned to the border patrol, which were in turn due to congressional delays in making the necessary budget appropriations and to INS difficulties in hiring and training the appropriate staff. It is also attributable to an expansion of the functions of the border patrol in two major areas, both of which were unanticipated by IRCA: the involvement of border patrol personnel in employers' education and enforcement activities and the designation in 1986 of the INS border patrol as the prime "interdictor" of drug traffic across U.S. land borders.

Although many of IRCA's provisions remain to be implemented and/ or vigorously enforced, the debate about the nature and magnitude of its outcomes and its overall effectiveness in reducing illegal immigration has already begun. We now turn to these questions of effects.

Notes

1. Throughout this chapter, "to date" generally means as of February 1989, unless noted otherwise.

2. All data referred to in this subsection were obtained directly from the INS, unless otherwise specified.

3. Throughout this report we alternatively use the terms *legalization* and *legalization programs* to refer to both (1) the regular legalization program (LAWs) for undocumented immigrants residing in the country since 1982 or earlier; and (2) the Special Agricultural Worker's program (SAWs) for undocumented immigrants having worked in perishable agricultural during a specified period of time.

4. Applicants also paid for services such as fingerprinting, photographing, and medical examinations.

5. The INS used its upper-range estimate of 3.9 million applications to design the capacity of its application intake facilities and personnel requirements and its lower-range estimate of 2.0 million applications to set the fee amount.

6. This border entry program was begun by the INS in summer 1987, partly in response to concerns expressed by agricultural growers about potential "labor shortages." It was made permanent through November 1988 by congressional action (PL 100–202) on December 22, 1987 (Martin and Taylor, 1988).

7. Legislation was considered in Congress to extend the legalization program deadline for applications, but no action was taken. Depending on the outcome of the ongoing litigation, the application period for specified classes of undocumented aliens may be extended.

8. Based on the 2.6 million applications entered on the INS computer files as of January 1989, most applications filed through a lawyer were for the LAWs program.

9. For each applicant the beginning of the 18-month period coincides with the date of his or her initial application.

10. The INS is still developing the regulations to guide the transition from temporary to permanent residence for SAW applicants. Unlike LAWs applicants, the former are exempt from meeting any civic or language requirements.

11. To be eligible for permanent residence on December 1989, SAW applicants had to have worked 90 workdays for each year in 1984, 1985, and 1986. These applicants represent about 13 percent of all SAW applicants, and thus it is likely that fewer than 200,000 SAWs applicants will be eligible for permanent residence in December 1989.

12. A comprehensive study of the first 30 months of IRCA's implementation was initiated by the Program for Research on Immigration Policy and will be completed in 1989 (see discussion later in this chapter).

13. As a means to partially support the QDEs' outreach efforts.

14. An additional 10,900 applications for SAWs were filed with the U.S. consulates in Mexico.

15. These public information campaigns have not been assessed. Two limited localized surveys (North and Portz, 1988; NuStats, 1987) found that in excess of 90 percent of the undocumented aliens whom they interviewed were aware of the LAW program. See section on "Legalization" in chapter 5 for a discussion of participation in the legalization program.

16. The LAWs regulations were not released until five days prior to the opening of the LAWs applications on May 4, 1987. Proposed regulations were published on March 19, 1989.

17. Such regional and district variations are being studied by the Program for Research on Immigration Policy (see chapter 5).

18. The INS initiated 634 major fraud investigations and 168 major fraud prosecutions related to the SAW program in FY 1988 (U.S. Office of Management and Budget, 1989). By December of 1988, INS had obtained 115 convictions.

19. Strictly, the act required a six-month education period beginning December 1, 1986.

20. The postponement was requested because of a delay in incorporating public comments in the design of the I–9 form, prompting concern that employers were not fully aware of IRCA's requirements (GAO, 1987d).

21. The INS reports that this target was exceeded (GAO, 1988e).

22. For a discussion of the extent of sanctions activities, see the section on "Employers" later in this chapter.

23. Specified circumstances generally mean if the employer had not received an educational or other INS visit and no egregious factors were present, such as willful failure to complete I–9s or willful hiring of undocumented workers.

24. The term *interior apprehensions* generally refers to apprehensions made at places of residence or employment of undocumented aliens. Reduced enforcement in this area is consistent with the "cooperative" stance adopted by the INS, as noted earlier, and a desire to encourage applications to the legalization programs.

25. As of June 1, 1989, there were no agents still in training, and 632 staff were performing other supporting functions. There were 4,594 border patrol staff by June 1989.

26. In FY 1987, INS seizures of narcotics and other merchandise had increased three-fold relative to FY 1986 (INS, 1988a).

27. In November 1988, the INS requested a review of the procedures guiding the DOL–INS interface.

28. Western growers made little use of the H–2A predecessor program, the H–2 program. The DOL reported that during this period its primary concern and that of its affiliated state and local agencies was to try to advise migrant workers to avoid labor surplus areas and to direct them to areas where work might be available. It also provided special funding to local agencies to provide immigration aid and support services to migrant workers adversely affected by the drought.

29. To date, no review of the activities generated by the SLIAG and SAVE provisions are available. The early experience with SAVE pilot projects (begun in 1984) was reviewed by the GAO (see GAO, 1987b; 1987c). The role of SLIAG in assisting LAWs program temporary residents to apply and qualify for "permanent residence" is currently dominating the state and local debate about the second phase of the legalization program, focusing on issues of use of public and nonprofit institutions' space, teaching, and funding capacity to meet the needs.

30. The other states are Connecticut, Delaware, Kansas, Maine, Massachusetts, Montana, New Hampshire, Vermont, and Virginia.

31. In contrast, Illinois and California have elected not to do so or have terminated their involvement because of budget constraints (GAO, 1987d; State of California, 1988).

32. It is noteworthy that IRCA does not cover wages, promotions, employee benefits, or other terms and conditions of employment already covered by Title VII of the Civil Rights Act of 1964.

33. Unless otherwise noted, this subsection relies primarily on two studies: GAO (1988h) and New York State Inter-Agency Task Force (NYS, 1988). The reader should be aware of several limitations of these surveys. Responses to the GAO survey were relatively low in some industries (particularly from those with a higher dependence on undocumented labor, such as garment, food processing, and agricultural industries). Response rates also were smaller for smaller-sized firms. The New York State survey was limited to the New York City metropolitan area.

34. Data collection for the GAO survey was done primarily during the first quarter of 1988, and for the New York State survey in mid-1988.

35. The GAO conducted a second survey of employers in spring 1989.

36. In a 1987–88 survey of 103 employers in southern California, at least half of whom had been inspected by the INS prior to IRCA, 93 percent reported compliance with the I–9 requirements. 96 percent of a sample of employees in the survey reported they had been asked to show documents required by IRCA (Cornelius, 1988).

37. Although not generally the practice, the INS may give one notice of intent to fine for each employee in violation. For instance, one employer in New Orleans accounted for 126 such notices.

38. In addition, the INS is working on the development of one card for aliens to use for work authorization purposes.

Chapter Five

ASSESSING IRCA'S EFFECTS

To assess IRCA's effects we must aim, ultimately, to answer three basic questions:

1. Has the law met its objectives?
2. What explains its success or failure—that is, how have outcomes been affected by its implementation, by the assumptions underlying its provisions, by the incentives it provided or failed to provide, or by unforeseen circumstances?
3. Has the law had major unintended effects, and are these desirable?

IRCA's overall goal was to legalize and regulate the flow of immigrant labor to the United States. Hence, its primary objectives have been (1) to curb, if not eliminate, the flow of undocumented immigrants into the country, and (2) to decrease the number of undocumented aliens residing in the United States. Clearly, the success or failure of IRCA will be measured largely against these chief objectives. However, IRCA should also be judged by its specific domestic and foreign impacts, some of which were explicitly addressed in IRCA's provisions and some of which were raised in congressional debates but not addressed in the legislation. The potentially adverse effects of IRCA domestically include:

□ Increased discrimination toward anyone looking or sounding foreign, regardless of immigration status;
□ The questionable adequacy of IRCA's SLIAG appropriations to meet the expected increased demand for state and local services by the legalized population, members of which are not eligible for major federal entitlement benefits for five years after receiving immigrant status;
□ Labor shortages, particularly in the perishable-products agricultural sector; and

□ Creation of a permanent "underclass" of undocumented aliens who arrived after 1982 and did not return to their country of origin.

The main potential domestic benefits expected from the new law are an enhancement of the job opportunities and wages of native-born and legal immigrant workers.

Two sets of international concerns have been expressed by Congress. One set arises from the possibility that the return of thousands of undocumented workers and the reduction of remittances to their families could have destabilizing economic and political effects for some sending countries (Mexico, especially). The other set of concerns relates to the predominantly unilateral treatment of immigration policy and the effects this might have on U.S. relations with other countries.

The first part of this chapter briefly describes the major evaluative studies of IRCA. The components of each study are outlined, along with the data-collection efforts in progress. Our focus is primarily, although not exclusively, on efforts that are national in scope.

The second part of the chapter draws on available completed studies to examine four issues that have occupied most of the public and analytical discussion over IRCA's effects: legalization, undocumented immigrants remaining in the country, discrimination, and illegal immigration. Because of the importance and complexity of the latter issue, we devote a full chapter to it (chapter 6). Several other important issues are not discussed here because findings regarding them have not yet been formally compiled. These issues, which will be addressed in subsequent yearbooks, include the amnestied population's demand for state and local services; the sectorial, localized, and labor market effects of the amnestied population and of employer sanctions; and international effects.

ONGOING EVALUATIVE STUDIES

Ongoing evaluative studies of IRCA fall into three major groups: studies mandated by Congress, studies that will result from the Program for Research on Immigration Policy, and studies of specific aspects of IRCA done by university centers, other nonprofit organizations, and governmental organizations.

Evaluations Mandated by Congress

Reflecting the controversy that preceded its passage, but atypical of new federal legislation, IRCA requires the president or specific federal agencies to evaluate many aspects of the implementation and effects of the new law, and for the first time, it mandates that a federal policy quantify the extent of its discriminatory effects in recruiting, hiring and firing, and employers' practices. Specific executive agencies are responsible for preparing these evaluations and in some cases are contracting for data collection or analytical services.

EFFECTS OF EMPLOYER SANCTIONS

The General Accounting Office, as noted earlier, is required to review the implementation and enforcement of employer sanctions to determine if such provisions (1) have been carried out satisfactorily, (2) have caused a pattern of discrimination against U.S. citizens or other eligible workers, and (3) have placed an unnecessary regulatory burden on employers. The law requires the GAO to issue three annual reports beginning in November 1987 and establishes procedures for Congress to repeal certain provisions of the law if GAO's third report, due in November 1989, finds a "widespread pattern" of discrimination caused "solely" by the law. To date, two reports have been issued (GAO, 1987d; 1988e).

In addition, the president is required to analyze the effects of employer sanctions on (1) the employment, wages, and working conditions of U.S. workers and on the economy of the United States, (2) the number of aliens entering the United States illegally or failing to maintain legal status after entry, and (3) the violations of terms and conditions of nonimmigrant visas by foreign visitors. The first such report is due in December 1989 and the last December 1991. In March 1989, the Department of Labor contracted with the Research Foundation of the State University of New York to collect information and analyze data to address the first question.

CHARACTERISTICS OF THE LAWS POPULATION

The president is required to describe the characteristics of the legalized population who entered the country prior to January 1, 1982. The INS has assumed responsibility for this report, which will include (1) geographical origins and manner of entry, (2) demographic characteristics, and (3) other general characteristics. This report is to be submitted to Congress in November 1989. Congress did not require a similar report for the population legalized under the Special Agricultural Workers (SAWs) program.

EFFECTS OF LAWS PROGRAM

The president is also required to evaluate the effects of the LAWs program. The departments of Labor and Health and Human Services, in conjunction with the INS, are sharing this responsibility, assessing (1) the effects of the legalization program on state and local governments and on public health and medical needs of individuals in the different regions of the United States, (2) the patterns of employment of the legalized population, and (3) the participation of legalized aliens in social service programs. This report is to be submitted to Congress in November 1992. The INS has selected a contractor, Westat, to survey applicants for legalization in order to address the foregoing areas. The survey was to be conducted in spring 1989. No decision has yet been made about a second wave of interviews prior to 1992.

Congress did not require a similar assessment of the alien population legalized under the SAWs program.

EFFECTS OF H–2A PROGRAM

The president is required to review the implementation of the temporary agricultural worker program (H–2A) to assess (1) the compliance of employers and foreign workers with the terms and conditions of the program; and (2) the effect of the program on the labor needs of U.S. agricultural employers and on the wages and working conditions of United States agricultural workers. The DOL submitted a first report to Congress in November 1988 (DOL, 1988). Subsequent reports covering the same issues are due every two years.

TRIENNIAL COMPREHENSIVE REPORT ON IMMIGRATION

In addition to the specific reports already noted, the president must submit to Congress a comprehensive immigration-impact report every three years. This report is to include: (1) the number of aliens admitted, paroled, or granted asylum during the relevant period; (2) the estimated number of undocumented aliens entering the country illegally or overstaying the duration of their visas; (3) a description of the effects of immigrants, refugees, asylees, and parolees on the economy; labor and housing markets; the educational system; social services; foreign policy; environmental quality and resources; the rate, size, and distribution of population growth in the United States; and (4) the impact on specific states and local units of government of high rates of immigration resettlement. Five-year projections on each of these topical areas are to be made.

The first triennial report was due to Congress on January 1, 1989. As of May 1989, the report had not been released publically.

RESEARCH SUPPORTED BY THE DEPARTMENT OF LABOR

Responding to IRCA and the mandate to issue a comprehensive immigration-impact statement every three years, in 1988 the Department of Labor established a new Division of Immigration Policy and Research within its Bureau of International Labor Affairs. This division is supporting research that addresses broad questions of immigration policy and effects. The research includes studies of the overall economic progress of immigrants, of displacement and/or complementarity between native-born workers and immigrants, of the geographic mobility of immigrants, and of the extent to which immigration may be a practical tool for labor market policy.

Program for Research on Immigration Policy

In February 1988, The RAND Corporation and The Urban Institute established the Program for Research on Immigration Policy, with initial support from the Ford Foundation.[1] During its first two years, the program is focusing on important domestic and international issues raised by IRCA, primarily through studies of the law's implementation and of its outcomes. The research design links the two kinds of studies, enabling the program to trace how implementation influences outcomes.

The implementation studies constitute an integrated project for assessing how effectively IRCA's nominal policies are put into practice; how they influence the behavior of immigrants, employers, state and local governments, and service providers; and how much of IRCA's success or failure results from its design and how much from the way it was implemented. The project is assessing IRCA implementation in eight major metropolitan areas that have been heavily affected by immigration and in agricultural areas of key states.

The outcomes studies are estimating IRCA's social, demographic, and economic effects—both domestic and international.

On the domestic side the program is assessing three outcomes: (1) IRCA's effects on illegal immigration; (2) IRCA's effects on U.S. agriculture; and (3) the numbers of illegal aliens who remain after legalization and how they attempt to cope. The third study will involve developing improved data collection methods.

On the international side, the program is studying two outcomes: (1) the ways in which the Mexican and U.S. policy elite view IRCA's effects on U.S.–Mexican relations and (2) what their response implies for future relations and policy. The program is also providing partial support for a study conducted by the Center for U.S.–Mexico Studies (University of California, San Diego), which is described in the next section.

The Program for Research on Immigration Policy seeks also to inform immigration policymaking and research related to IRCA's effects and outcomes through conferences, workshops, seminars and other informational activities. In 1989, it is holding three international conferences, assembling researchers, policymakers and program administrators from the United States and countries affected by U.S. immigration policy. Its first conference was held in May 1989 in Guadalajara, Mexico, and focused on the international effects of IRCA, and its second was held in July 1989 in Washington, D.C., focusing on illegal immigration since the passage of IRCA.

Other IRCA-Related Research Activities

A number of other university-based centers and nonprofit organizations, as well as governmental organizations, have initiated research projects addressing specific aspects of the implementation or outcomes of IRCA. The projects identified here are not necessarily a comprehensive list. Our second annual report will seek to inventory all evaluative efforts currently underway.

The *Center for Immigration Studies* is assessing IRCA's effects on perishable crop agriculture. The study seeks to determine the extent to which IRCA is (1) reducing the number of undocumented aliens in agriculture; (2) helping meet the labor needs of perishable crop agriculture; and (3) affecting wages and working conditions of legal workers. Completion of the study is expected in spring 1990.

TransCentury Development Associates is analyzing the operations of IRCA's two amnesty programs. An interim report was issued in March 1988 (North and Portz, 1988). A final report was to be submitted in spring 1989.

The *Center for U.S. Mexico Studies at the University of California at San Diego* is studying the effects of IRCA, using data from three rural communities in the Mexican states of Zacatecas, Jalisco, and Michoacán. The study's objectives are to estimate changes in: (1) the magnitude of temporary and permanent emigration from Mexico; (2)

the characteristics of the migrants and nonmigrants; (3) the propensity to migrate in the future (both among recurrent migrants and people who have not yet migrated to the United States); (4) remittances from migrants in the United States to people back in Mexico; and (5) use of income earned in the United States.

The center is also completing a pre-/post-IRCA study of the behavior of a sample of about 85 employers and their immigrant employees in southern California to assess: (1) changes in employers' production behavior; (2) participation in the legalization program; and (3) changes in labor force participation of immigrants.

The *Colegio de la Frontera del Norte* (COLEF) is studying how illegal immigrants attempt to enter the United States from Mexico. COLEF's Canyon Zapata Project has two major data collection components: (1) interviewing, at regular intervals and at five locations along the U.S.–Mexican border, a sample of people who intend to migrate from Mexico to the United States (10,000 interviews had been completed as of October 1988), and (2) daily photographing and subsequent counting of aspiring migrants concentrating in Canyon Zapata, located in Baja California near Tijuana.

The *Institute for Research on Poverty at the University of Wisconsin* is analyzing the work behavior and use of welfare of previously undocumented aliens amnestied under IRCA because of continuous residence in the United States since 1982. Two datasets will be used in this study: (1) information derived from the form filled out by all applicants for legal status and (2) the responses from the earlier-mentioned cross-sectional survey of a sample of applicants, for spring 1989.

The *Commission for the Study of International Migration and Cooperative Economic Development*, established by IRCA, is examining the conditions in sending countries that lead to undocumented migration to the United States, in order to recommend reciprocal economic measures aimed at easing those conditions. Although not focusing directly on these effects, the commission's research activities touch on issues related to these effects—including bilateral relations between the United States and sending countries, the flow and use of remittances, job development in sending countries, and the relationship between development and migration. The commission is required to report its findings to the president and Congress in February 1990.

The *Bureau of the Census* is continuing its efforts to update and enhance the reliability of its estimates of the number of undocumented aliens residing in the United States. It is now developing a 1980 estimate of the size of this population based on the 1988 Current Population Survey (CPS).

The *Immigration and Naturalization Service* is estimating the change over time in the number of nonimmigrant visa holders who have remained (illegally) in this country beyond the time period authorized by their visas.

Finally, the *National Council of La Raza* is working on a study of the effectiveness of IRCA, which was to be completed in summer 1989.

The mandated and nonmandated evaluative activities listed here constitute an ambitious and unprecedented set of efforts to assess the implementation and effects of a significant new law that potentially may affect every worker in the United States and many workers in other countries. Even so, at least two key policy questions are not being adequately addressed.

The first concerns the labor mobility and service needs and use of the population legalized under the SAWs program. As discussed further in the next section, the number of applicants for this program exceeds all expectations. For this reason, and because those legalized under SAW may work in any sector of the economy, it will be critical to gain an understanding of these individuals' mobility, employment, and service needs so as to assess the eventual effects of IRCA on labor markets and demand for services in high-impact areas.

The second key question concerns the numbers and behavioral patterns of those undocumented aliens who were in this country when IRCA was passed and have stayed, or who have come since 1986 and have stayed. This issue is examined in the next subsection which discusses the known effects of IRCA to date.[2]

EFFECTS TO DATE

This section of the chapter draws on findings from the completed studies to discuss three issues that have dominated the debate over IRCA's effects: legalization, undocumented immigrants remaining in the country, and discrimination. Before turning to the discussion, some words of caution are in order. Findings to date and our interpretation of them should be considered highly tentative for several reasons, both administrative and nonadministrative.

The most obvious administrative reason is that IRCA's numerous programs and provisions are being implemented over five years. Since substantial pieces of the law are not yet in place, we can hardly make definitive assessments of its implementation or effects.

A second administrative reason is that IRCA has catapulted the federal agencies and the nation's employers who must implement its provisions into unfamiliar roles. Both must master the complex provisions, rules, and regulations that apply to them, and the agencies must also develop relevant institutional capabilities to carry out their missions. What occurs while these adjustments are being made will not fully typify agencies' and employers' actions after this period.

A third administrative consideration is the discretion Congress has given agencies in interpreting IRCA's intent and implementing its provisions. This discretionary latitude leaves the agencies' decisions open to legal challenges and pressure from interest groups. Several decisions have already been challenged and modified and more challenges are likely. Consequently, implementation strategies and resource allocations among IRCA-related activities are continuously evolving.

Regarding nonadministrative reasons, the first is that IRCA challenges practices that have developed over more than two decades. Illegal immigration has benefited many groups, and reform is bound to meet resistance (Rosenberg and Mamer, 1987). At the outset, many employers and workers may adopt a wait-and-see attitude, persisting in their pre-IRCA practices. The extent and duration of this behavior will depend on how effective enforcement is. As noted earlier, enforcement is only just beginning.

Second, lack of reliable data inhibits measuring and interpreting IRCA's effects. Certain provisions of IRCA encourage new data collection and development of new methodologies to study illegal immigration. However, few such efforts have been completed, and even when they are complete, one data problem will persist: the absence of reliable data about the number of undocumented residents, their behavior, and the behavior of employers prior to the implementation of the new law. This problem plagued the prepassage debate and may preclude unequivocal statements about IRCA's success for the foreseeable future.

Even given these caveats, we think the following review of available evidence provides a good indication of what is known. We have been careful to rely on government and university-based studies, rather than on the anecdotal assessments appearing almost daily in the print media.

Legalization

IRCA's legalization programs are the largest ever implemented, with approximately 3 million applicants—1.7 million under the LAWs program and 1.3 million under the SAWs program. Until now, Venezuela had implemented the largest program, with 350,000 undocumented residents seeking and receiving legalization (Carrasco, 1988). Although the application period stipulated under IRCA is closed, additional applications are still being taken as a result of court decisions. To date, 1.6 million applications have been approved, with approval rates running about 98 percent for the LAWs program and 94 percent for the SAWs program. Approval rates on the remaining applications are expected to be somewhat lower.[3] However, it is not unreasonable to expect that more than 2.7 million undocumented aliens will eventually be approved for temporary residence.

Figure 5.1 displays the LAWs and SAWs applicants' country of origin, state of residence, and demographic characteristics. The majority of applicants to both programs are Mexicans, reside in California, are between the ages of 15 and 34, and are males. Four out of 10 are married. Only in gender do applicants to the LAWs program differ significantly from applicants to the SAWs program. Eighty-three percent of SAWs applicants are male, compared to 57 percent for the LAWs program. Most countries of origin produced more LAWs than SAWs applicants, the three exceptions being Haiti, India, and Pakistan. Similarly, almost all states received more LAWs than SAWs applications, with one exception, Florida, which received twice as many SAW as LAW applications.

The success of IRCA's legalization programs will be debated for some time to come and there may never be a consensus on their effectiveness. The main reason for this, as already stressed, is that no one knows and will ever know for certain how many eligible undocumented aliens there were in the first place. Current best estimates of their number when the amnesty application period opened in 1987 program range from 1.3 million to 2.7 million for the LAWs program and from 250,000 to 350,000 for the SAWs program.[4]

Those estimates yield a LAWs participation rate ranging from 63 percent to 100 percent.[5] This compares favorably with the experience of amnesty programs in other countries, where applications have typically run 30 percent to 80 percent of expected applications (Carrasco, 1988). In turn, the SAWs program was "successful" far beyond expectations, raising widespread speculations about a high rate of fraudulent applications.[6]

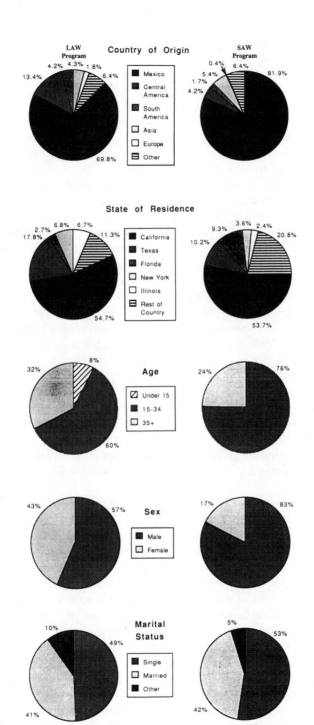

Figure 5.1 SELECTED CHARACTERISTICS OF APPLICANTS TO IRCA LEGALI-
ZATION PROGRAMS

Another indicator of success is the extent to which the profile of applicants matches that of undocumented aliens counted in the 1980 Census. Overall, the distribution by country of origin and state of residence of applicants for legalization matches the distribution of undocumented persons who were counted by the 1980 census (see figure 5.2). There are exceptions, however. By this measure, Europeans and Asian applicants for legalization are underrepresented, as are applications from the state of New York.

There are at least three potential reasons for these exceptions. First, between 1980 and 1987, there might have been greater attrition among European and Asian undocumented workers, due to higher departure rates or higher rates of change in immigration status. Second, outreach and public information efforts to Asians and Europeans may not have been as effective as those to other groups (Meissner and Papademetriou, 1988). Third, there may have been regional differences in attitudes among the undocumented aliens and in levels of effort among INS regional districts. Available data does not permit us to sort out the possible effects of these factors.

Observers of the legalization program have pointed out several possible disincentives for participation by some eligible individuals—some due to the design of the program and some due to its administration. The most prominent in the first category include (1) fear of the INS, (2) documentation requirements, (3) complex eligibility requirements, (4) cost of application, and (5) the exclusion of family members from legalization unless they were eligible in their own right.

The first two of these disincentives appear not to have been major deterrents. About 7 out of 10 applicants applied directly to the INS, rather than through qualified designated entities (QDEs) or through a lawyer, suggesting little fear of the INS;[7] and, as noted earlier, the INS appears to have been increasingly more flexible over time about documentation requirements. But early inflexibility may have discouraged some applicants, who therefore may not have returned to apply, and there have been court challenges of some of the INS's documentation requirements; thus, it remains to be seen how many eligibles might in fact have been discouraged on these accounts.

The deterrent effect of the family unity issue is difficult to assess. IRCA legalization legislation was designed to benefit individuals with specified characteristics, not families. Many saw the exclusion of spouses and children of eligible undocumented aliens as a major deterrent, at least in the early months of the application period. This

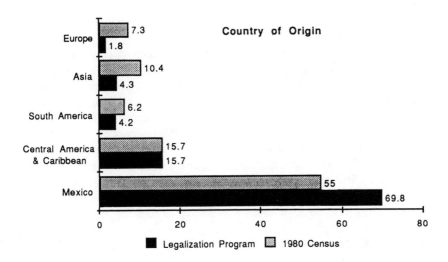

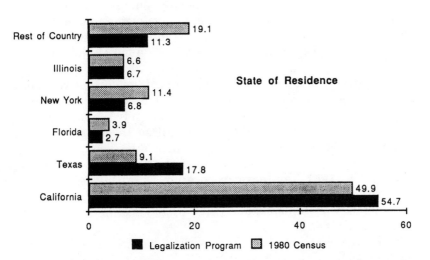

Figure 5.2 DISTRIBUTION BY COUNTRY OF ORIGIN AND STATE OF RESIDENCE
OF APPLICANTS FOR LEGALIZATION AND OF UNDOCUMENTED PER-
SONS COUNTED BY 1980 U.S. CENSUS

issue was widely debated in the public forum and, indeed, may have discouraged some from applying.[8]

As noted earlier, participation in the legalization programs may have been affected by administrative factors, including (1) delays in issuing rules and regulations, (2) changes over time in access and regulations guiding eligibility, (3) shortcomings in the public information campaign, and (4) variations in practices among INS regions and districts. One localized survey by North and Portz (1988), done midway through the legalization program, suggested that confusion about eligibility and lack of documentation were two main reasons why eligible individuals were opting out of the program at that time. Respondents did not identify fear of the INS, concern about family unity question, or lack of money as major factors.[9]

Remaining Undocumented Population

Assessing the success of the legalization programs by comparing the actual number of applicants to the estimates of the number of eligible undocumented immigrants is unsatisfactory because of the unreliability of the latter estimate. Consequently, attention has turned to measuring the size of the remaining undocumented population to obtain a more reliable indicator. This measure is a potential indicator not only of the effectiveness of the legalization but also of the IRCA legislation as a whole.

Congress expected that some undocumented immigrants who failed to achieve legalized status would eventually leave voluntarily if they could not find work. To date, just as there is only limited evidence about the effect of IRCA on illegal immigration, there is no evidence that any significant number of undocumented illegals ineligible for amnesty have departed. Anticipating potentially large numbers of returnees in 1987, the Mexican government established an interministerial commission to handle the reintegration of returnees.[10] No program was implemented (GAO, 1988b) and there seems to be no need for it yet.

Undocumented aliens who might still be in the United States fall into four subgroups: (1) those statutorily eligible for legalization who opted not to apply for whatever reason; (2) those who arrived between January 1, 1982, and November 6, 1986, and can keep the job they held prior to November 6, 1986;[11] (3) those who arrived prior to November 6, 1986, but were not statutorily eligible for legalization or "grandfathering" because they were not employed at that time; (4) those who arrived after November 6, 1986. Subject to the assumptions made, the aggregate size of this "residual" population might range from less than 500,000 to in excess of 2.2 million.[12] It would be desirable to obtain a reliable count of this population and to document IRCA's effects on their living conditions in the United States.[13]

There are at least two reasons to expect that many (possibly most) ineligible workers will remain here. First, the growing disparities in job opportunities and wages between the United States and the various countries of origin, as well as political and social unrest in some of these countries make undocumented immigrants unlikely to leave voluntarily, even if their job opportunities or wages fall here. A second reason is the family ties that some remaining undocumented individuals have with legal or IRCA-legalized immigrants. As noted earlier, 40 percent of the applicants for legalization are married. Those "grandfathered" by IRCA have the option of remaining with their employers. Others who remain have several adjustment options available—increased self-employment; accepting employment in firms that are willing to risk sanctions, possibly on substandard terms; accepting longer periods of unemployment or underemployment; and/or obtaining fraudulent documents, thereby satisfying, albeit illegally, the employer requirements. Many ineligible workers have relatives here, some of whom have been legalized, from whom they may get some support. Hardships are likely to fall more heavily on family members remaining behind in the sending countries, as the remittances they receive decrease or become more irregular.

Discrimination

Congress was concerned that employers' fear of sanctions for hiring unauthorized aliens might lead them to avoid hiring, or that they would otherwise discriminate against U.S. citizens or legal aliens "who look or sound foreign." Thus, it prohibited employers with four or more employees from discriminating in recruitment, hiring, or discharging, on the basis of country of origin or citizenship; it created an Office of Special Counsel on Employment Discrimination (OSC) in the Department of Justice to investigate and prosecute charges; and it charged the General Accounting Office with determining whether IRCA is causing a pattern of discrimination against authorized workers. Congress also gave itself the power to use expedited procedures to repeal the employer sanctions and antidiscrimination provisions if the GAO finds either a "widespread pattern" or alternatively "no significant pattern" of discrimination caused "solely" by the sanctions provision by the third year of IRCA implementation, (U.S. Congress, 1986).

As of November 1988, after two years of IRCA implementation, the GAO concluded that the data on discrimination it has collected or reviewed do not establish "a pattern of discrimination caused by employer sanctions." Nevertheless, the GAO stated that policymakers should be concerned about the potentially discriminatory practices of some employers and that federal agencies should provide the public with more information about the act. Anticipating its third and last mandated report on this issue, the GAO also warned that "methodological problems in measuring discrimination and tracing its causes (to employer sanctions) . . . may preclude from determining whether a pattern of discrimination exists" (GAO, 1988e).

TYPE AND INCIDENCE OF POTENTIAL DISCRIMINATION

Studies by the GAO and other entities[14] have documented several forms of potentially discriminatory behavior by employers:

☐ Preference given to U.S. citizens;
☐ Hiring of citizens or green-card holders only;
☐ Refusal to hire or to pre-screen anyone who looks foreign;
☐ Failure to recognize authorized documents;
☐ Requiring documentation only from persons looking or sounding foreign;
☐ Dismissal or threats of dismissal of "grandfathered" and other authorized workers;
☐ Loss of seniority or benefits;
☐ Preference given to undocumented workers;
☐ Requiring too many documents or only specific documents from everyone;
☐ Applying higher standards of documentation or employment qualifications from individuals looking or sounding foreign; and
☐ Hiring only after appropriate documentation has been provided, although the law requires that job seekers be hired without regard to their immediate ability to produce acceptable documentation.

In addition, discriminatory practices have been reported against undocumented aliens in the forms of requiring them to compensate employers for the costs of INS sanctions; lower wages; and/or withholding payment of wages.

The extent of these practices and the number of individuals affected by them are not reliably known. Two surveys of employers in 1988 (GAO, 1988e; NYS, 1988) and ongoing monitoring by immigration rights groups, however, provide suggestive evidence (CHIRLA, 1988; GAO, 1988e; NYS, 1988). These studies also suggest that inadequate knowledge or understanding of the law's requirements may be the primary causes of these practices.[15]

In its survey of more than 3,000 employers nationwide, for example, the GAO found that "one in every six employers who were aware of the law may have begun or increased the practice of (1) hiring only U.S. citizens or (2) asking only foreign-looking persons for work authorizations (GAO, 1988e). About 5 percent of the employers in this survey had a policy of hiring U.S. citizens only.

In a survey of 400 employers by the New York State Inter-Agency Task Force on Immigration Affairs (1988), no definite case of citizens-only discrimination was found, but about 2 percent of employers reported having a policy of hiring green-card holders only, and 1.7 percent of employers screened out workers looking foreign.

In this case, as in many other instances of potential discriminatory practices, misunderstanding of the law's requirements may have motivated some employers to "play it safe." Indeed, as indicated in chapter 4, 20 percent of employers surveyed by the GAO (1988e) reported they were unclear about their authority to hire a U.S. citizen rather than an authorized alien when both are equally qualified.[16]

Selective screening (i.e., asking documentation from only some workers or having different documentation requirements for different workers) was reported by 7.4 percent of employers in the GAO (1988e) survey and 6.9 percent of employers in the NYS (1988) survey.[17] In the latter survey, it represents 4 percent of all jobs.

Termination of "grandfathered" and other authorized workers and loss of seniority and/or benefits[18] constitute the majority of charges that have been reported to immigrants'-rights organizations and to the OSC (GAO, 1988e). Reasons for terminating authorized workers include employers not recognizing or accepting authorized documentation, and occasional accusations of employees using fraudulent documents. Cases of loss of seniority may involve both employers who believe that this termination/rehire would protect them from discovery that an employee used to be undocumented and employers who may be "taking advantage" of an employee's past use of an alias or false document.

In spite of efforts by the INS and other agencies to inform and educate employers of the law's requirements, about one in five of the employers surveyed in the New York City metropolitan area (NYS, 1988) did not know about all alternative forms of authorized documentation, and, in particular, less-frequent types of documents such as those provided by the INS to refugees and asylum applicants.

Nor did many of them know of the procedural requirement of "hiring first and checking documents later." Two-thirds of employers who hired new employees since November 1987 reported that they require documents before the first day of work (NYS, 1988), in violation of the INS regulation that new employees have 3 days to show they have sent for the documents and 21 days to submit them to the employer.

The practice of requiring documentation prior to hiring may simply be a continuation of past practices. The survey results indicate, for example, that employers who never heard of the I–9 requirements were more likely to require documentation from their prospective hirees before hiring them than those who knew about IRCA's requirements. But the incidence of employers deciding not to hire an individual because documents could not be produced fast enough was much higher among employers who knew about IRCA (12 percent) than among those who did not (1 percent).

Some have also argued that IRCA's documentation requirements might adversely affect native-born workers such as youths, women, and minorities who have not in the past needed the kind of documents now required by the law. The NYS (1988) survey of employers indicated that one out of three had experiences with employees who had difficulty getting documentation. Those who knew of IRCA's requirements had experienced a higher incidence of such cases than those who did not.

All these issues deserve further study.

FORMAL CHARGES OF DISCRIMINATION

Typically, only a small percentage of potentially discriminatory practices results in charges being brought through the appropriate enforcement agencies, in this case, the OSC and the EEOC.[19] As of February 1989, 454 charges had been filed with the OSC,[20] with the bulk (40 percent) in California and Texas, Illinois, and New York accounting for 10 percent each.

In the roughly 18-month period from IRCA's passage to June 1988, employer sanctions could not be issued without warning. During that period, the OSC had received 141 complaints. In the 9 months from June 1988 through February 1989, the number of complaints filed has increased twofold, with the number of charges brought to the OSC increasing steadily over time.

A review by the GAO of 119 charges filed with the OSC as of May 1988 (the most recent date for which estimates are available), indicates that half of the charges involved fired individuals, and 40 percent involved individuals who were not hired (GAO, 1988e). To date, the OSC has closed 57 percent of the charges filed. Nearly four out of five were dismissed because of lack of jurisdiction, no reasonable cause to believe discrimination occurred, or insufficient evidence to prosecute. The remaining cases were generally settled in favor of the plaintiff, who usually received back pay and reinstatement.

Finally, 40 charges have been filed by the OSC or by other parties with the Administrative Law Judge. Eleven have been closed, most in settlements prior to trial.

In addition to processing charges, the OSC has the discretion to initiate investigations on its own initiative.[21] The OSC reports having initiated several hundred independent investigations, particularly in the defense and airline industries, which were advertising "citizens"-only positions. Most of the companies involved agreed to change their practices, opening up thousands of jobs previously closed to qualified aliens.

PROTECTION OF REMAINING UNDOCUMENTED WORKERS

How much protection do remaining undocumented workers have against discrimination and other unfair labor practices (Merino, 1988)? Under current U.S. law, undocumented workers retain formal employment rights and are covered by the National Labor Relations Act, the Occupational Safety and Health Act, and the Fair Labor Standards Act. However, IRCA may have made them more vulnerable and possibly less likely to bring charges under these laws than they were in the pre-IRCA period. IRCA addresses the question of discrimination on the bases of country of origin or citizenship for the native, legal immigrant, and amnestied population. It does not cover the undocumented workers remaining in the United States. The EEOC has taken the position that Title VII (as opposed to IRCA) protects undocumented workers from discrimination based on race, color, sex, national origin, or religion (GAO, 1988e). Yet, the GAO (1988e) reports that the EEOC has not yet determined the remedies available to such workers under Title VII. IRCA is reportedly unclear and, thus, the courts may yet have to decide whether exempt (grandfathered) aliens are covered by IRCA's antidiscrimination provisions.

CONCLUSION

The preceding discussion offers ample support for the notion that it is too early to draw definitive conclusions either about IRCA's effectiveness as a whole or about the success of its individual provisions. It also remains uncertain whether some of the effects noted in this chapter—in particular, those concerning discriminatory practices—will be long lasting. Many provisions, as emphasized throughout this chapter, are not fully implemented and/or not fully enforced, and the implementing agencies are continuously adjusting their own practices as they gain more operating experience.

Many studies—some mandated by Congress and some undertaken with financial support from private foundations—promise to offer answers to some of the effects questions raised by IRCA. Two issues, however, are currently not receiving the attention justified by their importance. The first is the question of IRCA's effects on the size and behavior of the undocumented population remaining in the country. And the second concerns the labor mobility of the unexpectedly large 1.3 million workers legalized under the SAWs program. (Congress provided that this latter question would be addressed for the LAWs population, but not for the SAWs population.) To gain reliable answers to both questions would require the development and use of survey techniques that cater to these difficult-to-identify populations—an expensive proposition. Still, the answers to these questions are critical to eventually assessing the effects of IRCA on illegal immigration, on labor markets, and on demand for services in high-impact areas.

Notes

1. For more information about the program see the Appendix to this monograph.

2. Throughout this chapter, the term "to date" refers to February 1989.

3. This is expected to be particularly true in the SAWs programs where fraud is suspected to have been more extensive.

4. All estimates of the size of the population eligible for the LAWs program when applications were taken start from the same Census Bureau estimate of 2.06 million illegal aliens counted in the 1980 Census. From there, estimates vary according to the assumptions made, first, by adjusting the base 1980 estimate to an estimate of the number of undocumented persons residing in the United States on January 1, 1982,

and, second, by adjusting this latter estimate to May 5, 1987, to account for (1) undocumented reasons not counted by the 1980 Census; (2) new entries, departures, and changes in immigration status between 1980 and 1982; (3) departures, changes in immigration status, and discontinuity in stays and other limiting IRCA eligibility provisions between 1982 and 1987. Recent estimates for undocumented persons in the United States prior to January 1, 1982, range from 2.7 million to 3.8 million, and estimates of losses from 1982 to 1987 range from 10 percent to 50 percent (Hoefer, 1988b).

5. The fact that the lower-bound estimate of individuals eligible for the legalization program is smaller than the actual number of applicants is, in our opinion, more a reflection of the unreliability of the estimate than a suggestion of extensive fraud in that program. Also, it is well documented that participation in entitlement programs that require an application to be filed—such as food stamps, welfare, and even Medicaid—typically fall short of 100 percent participation by eligibles.

6. There have been many anecdotal instances of alleged fraudulent applications under the SAWs program, ranging from applicants not knowing even the most elementary basics of the crops they presumably had harvested to the purchase of fraudulent affidavits "documenting" work in agriculture during the required period. To date, few such cases of fraud have been successfully prosecuted by the government.

7. Some of those who applied directly at an INS office received prior information, guidance, and/or counseling from QDEs, enabling them to file on their own.

8. Early in the legalization process, the INS noted that it lacked the legislative mandate to give massive "extended voluntary departure" to ineligible family members, as some were advocating. But it also noted that the information obtained through the application process could not and would not be used to apprehend or ask family members to leave (Norton, 1988).

9. Because those interviewed were users of QDEs or were identified through the users of QDEs, this survey may well underestimate the role played by these concerns. Those opting out for these reasons may have been less likely to go to a QDE for help in the first place.

10. Also, the Mexican government's Consejo Nacional de Poblacion (CONAPO) had prepared a contingency plan to accommodate the expected large flow of returnees.

11. These "grandfathered" individuals are exempt from submitting documentation, and their employers are exempt from sanction. However, if apprehended by the INS they are not exempt from deportation.

12. The upper-bound estimate assumes 170,000 new permanent arrivals of undocumented aliens annually since 1982 (the Bureau of the Census estimate) and adds to it the balance between the upper-bound estimate of those eligible for amnesty (2.7 million) and those who applied (1.7 million). The lower-bound estimate also assumes 170,000 new arrivals annually since 1982, but then assumes that practically all those eligible for legalization under LAWs actually applied and that up to 60 percent of the SAWs applicants are individuals who arrived after 1982 and applied for legalization under that program. The National Council of La Raza (1988) estimates that the size of the remaining undocumented immigrant population in 1988 was 3.7 million.

13. The Program for Research on Immigration Policy plans to test the feasibility and cost of making such a count.

14. For instance, see NYS (1988) and Coalition for Humane Immigration Rights (CHIRLA, 1988).

15. As noted in chapter 4, the INS's initial educational efforts focused on the "authorized" workers provisions and not on the antidiscriminations provisions. The GAO (1988e) has recommended that greater efforts be made in this area. A federal inter-

agency task force, chaired by the OSC, was established to undertake an extensive public outreach program.

16. As mentioned earlier in this monograph, when both a U.S. citizen and an authorized alien are equally qualified, IRCA allows preference to be given to the first. However, an Equal Employment Opportunity Commission (EEOC) policy statement notes that such a practice is contrary to Title VII (of the Civil Rights' Act) antidiscrimination provisions based on national origin.

17. Because questions differed between the two surveys, these figures are not directly comparable.

18. Loss of seniority and/or benefits is not protected under IRCA, although it may be under Title VII of the Civil Rights Act.

19. The EEOC handles national origin discrimination charges filed under Title VII of the Civil Rights Act applying to employers with 10 employees or more.

20. The EEOC had received 175 IRCA-related national origin complaints as of December 1988, 80 percent of which were filed prior to June 1988.

21. In signing IRCA on November 6, 1986, the president expressed in a written statement his sense that the Special Counsel on Employment Discrimination should limit self-initiated investigations "to cases involving discrimination apparently caused by an employer's fear of liability under the [IRCA's] employer sanctions program."

Chapter Six

THE EFFECTS OF IRCA ON ILLEGAL IMMIGRATION

A principal objective of IRCA is to reduce the number of illegal immigrants coming to and residing in the United States. The law attempts to accomplish this through several means: (1) the legalization of many undocumented immigrants already residing here; (2) the prohibition of the hiring of undocumented workers and the enforcement of this prohibition; and (3) the authorization and appropriation of increased resources for enforcement activities by the border patrol. Included among the major tests of the effectiveness of IRCA will be the extent to which the flow of illegal immigrants into the country is actually reduced and the extent to which the size of the resident illegal alien population is diminished (beyond the reduction brought about by the legalization programs). This chapter examines the limited data now available to address these questions.

A number of caveats must be kept in mind in interpreting and evaluating evidence about the amount of illegal immigration to the United States. Heightened sensitivity to these caveats is critical, because questions about the number, characteristics, and impact of illegal immigrants are inevitably difficult to resolve and thus subject to speculative answers. In the 1970s, well-intentioned but nonanalytically-based assessments of the number of illegal aliens in the country proved ultimately to be inaccurate. Subsequent empirical estimates based on demographic analysis showed that these speculations substantially overstated the size of the population (Passel, 1986). In short, a lag occurred between the time illegal immigration began to be seen as a problem and the time that results of analytic studies began to provide research-based assessments of the size of the illegal population.[1]

This served in part to create an empirical vacuum in which exaggerated notions about the size of the undocumented population flourished (Passel, 1986). As the final report of the Select Commission on Immigration and Refugee Policy (1981) makes clear, however, many policymakers thought important reasons existed to try to curtail illegal immigration irrespective of the size of the undocumented population. However, the credibility of this position was sometimes undermined by excessively large claims concerning the size of the population. Now as efforts are being mounted to assess IRCA's effects on illegal immigration, it is important to foster conditions that can enable assessments that are as balanced and objective as possible. This means reviewing carefully some of the issues that complicate assessments of the size and flow of undocumented immigration.

ISSUES IN MEASURING ILLEGAL IMMIGRATION

Assessing whether illegal immigration into the United States has changed since the passage of IRCA is difficult for at least two reasons. One is that information on the size of the illegal population in the United States has always been hard to acquire. The second is that different types of undocumented migrants exist, each of which may be affected differently by IRCA.

The members of clandestine populations possess incentives *not* to identify themselves as illegal immigrants in censuses and other surveys. This makes it difficult and costly to identify, sample, interview, and enumerate individual illegal immigrants. Researchers interested in estimating the size of this population have therefore been forced to resort to other approaches, to rely on aggregate demographic rather than individual level analyses (see Bean, King, and Passel, 1985; Levine, Hill, and Warren, 1985). Such analytic studies appeared with increasing frequency in the late 1970s, after which a consensus began to emerge that the estimated number of undocumented immigrants in the United States fell below the range of numbers many observers had previously postulated. The estimated range for the number of undocumented aliens in the country in 1980 ran roughly between 2.5 million to 3.5 million, with undocumented Mexicans making up about 55 percent to 60 percent of the total (Passel, 1986). It is noteworthy that this range is consistent with the number of illegals applying for the LAWs and SAWs programs of IRCA (see chapter 5). However, the percentage of undocumented Mexicans is somewhat lower than the percentage of Mexicans applying for the legalization programs.

Another major reason why it is hard to assess illegal immigration is that there are different kinds of undocumented immigrants. The

Immigration and Naturalization Service distinguishes between two kinds of illegal immigrants: (1) persons who enter without any sort of legal visa (called "EWIs" because they "enter without inspection") and (2) persons who enter with legal visas but remain beyond the authorized time limit (called "visa-overstayers"), or persons who violate the terms of their temporary visas by taking a job (for example, persons with tourist visas). Such administrative distinctions are likely to be most useful when they reflect some important dimension of social and economic reality. In this case, the distinctions serve to demarcate reasonably well illegal immigrants who come from Mexico (almost all of whom are EWIs) versus those who come from other countries (almost all of whom are visa–overstayers).[2] EWIs and visa–abusers, however, cannot be operationally differentiated from one another in terms of their reasons for immigrating or their intended duration of residence—distinctions that are important for the formulation of sound immigration policy.

A more conceptually meaningful dichotomy appears in the migration literature, which draws a distinction between "sojourners" and "settlers" (Chavez, 1988). Based primarily on intended duration of residence in the country of destination, this conceptualization defines "settlers" as immigrants intending to reside in the United States permanently, and "sojourners" as migrants intending to return to their country of origin. In the case of the United States, some observers add still a third group of undocumented migrants—"commuters", persons who "do not actually live in the United States, but rather cross the U.S.–Mexican or U.S.–Canadian borders on a daily or almost daily basis to work in the United States" (Passel, 1986:183).

Obviously, it is difficult in practice to separate these three types of migrants—a problem that is exacerbated because individual migrants themselves may move back and forth from one category to another as their circumstances and intentions change. Nonetheless, it is important to keep the distinctions in mind to avoid confusion about the number of illegal migrants in the country. Although separate estimates of these groups have not been conducted, there is no reason, at least conceptually, why they could not be developed. Estimates about the size of the undocumented population in the country at a given time (called the "stock" of undocumented migrants) that include the members of all three groups would be larger than an estimate only of the stock of settlers. Similarly, the number crossing the border within a given period (the "flow" of undocumented migrants) would be larger than the stock. This is especially true when the number of sojourners and commuters is large relative to settlers, because the same individual may move back and forth across the border several times within a given period.

Also, the distinctions between types of migrants have implications for different policy issues and for assessments of IRCA's effects. Policy questions pertaining to labor market or labor force behavior might be best addressed based on data on the number of person-years worked in the United States, information that would be most useful if it included all three types of migrants. Certain social service providers might be interested in both settlers and sojourners. Assessments of IRCA's regular legalization program would involve examining a program applying to settlers, not to commuters or sojourners. Finally, cross-sectional estimates (or those taken at one specific time) of the illegal population would include fewer sojourners than the total number coming during the course of a year. If such estimates were used to predict the number of sojourners eligible to enroll in some program like the SAWs program, they would underestimate (perhaps substantially so) the number of enrollees.

EVALUATING RECENT DATA ABOUT POST-IRCA FLOWS

All of these considerations need to be taken into account in assessing the extent to which IRCA has affected illegal immigration to the United States. Has IRCA reduced the number of settlers? The number of sojourners? The number of commuters? Unfortunately, data are not available to estimate the sizes of each of these groups separately. Certainly, however, IRCA has reduced the number of *illegal* settlers by virtue of its legalization program. The SAWs program appears likely to have legalized substantial numbers of sojourners. But has the flow of sojourners and settlers coming into the country been reduced? That is, apart from changes in the size of the undocumented population already here, has IRCA reduced the numbers of illegal entrants coming to the United States during 1987 and 1988?

Some indication of an answer to this question may be provided by examining apprehensions data, one of the most frequently cited sources of information about undocumented immigration to the United States. Apprehensions statistics come from monthly tallies of the number of times persons entering the country illegally are apprehended by the U.S. border patrol or by other INS enforcement personnel. Over 90 percent of apprehensions (92 percent in fiscal years 1986 through 1988) are made by the border patrol, and of these, more than 99 percent consist of EWIs (according to our examination of unpublished INS tally sheets).

The number of apprehensions of illegal entrants has averaged over 1 million a year since 1982. These numbers seem to imply an illegal population of enormous size in the United States. But not only do such apprehensions include all three types of migrants noted previously, they also include persons who have been apprehended several times. Also, many persons apprehended during a given year return to Mexico before the end of the year. Thus, the number of apprehensions, which peaked at 1,609,278 in fiscal year 1986, substantially overstates the size of the illegal population that enters and remains in the country within any given year. Finally, apprehensions statistics alone could also lead to an understatement of the illegal flow of both sojourners and settlers, if many entrants go undetected.

Despite the possibility that many entrants go undetected, apprehensions statistics are of greatest value for making assessments of the flow rather than the stock of illegal immigrants. Data on apprehensions are particularly useful for gauging changes from one time period to another in the flow of undocumented entrants. Because almost all apprehensions are of Mexican aliens (92 percent in fiscal year 1987, the most recent year for which this statistic is available [INS, 1988a]), data on apprehensions pertain almost solely to questions of illegal immigration from Mexico. Although this prevents the data from being useful to assess changes in the flows of illegal migrants from other countries, they are nonetheless useful for gauging flows from Mexico, the country from which more than half of all the undocumented immigrants in the United States originate (Warren and Passel, 1987).

As a basis for assessing changes in illegal flows even from Mexico, however, a number of assumptions must be made before apprehensions data can be usefully interpreted. First, it is necessary to assume a constant level of INS enforcement effort, or to control for such effort, as noted in the paragraphs following. Second, it must be assumed that the proportion of illegal border crossings that goes undetected has remained relatively constant over time. Third, it must be assumed that other variables that might affect the number of illegal crossings do not appreciably explain any changes in apprehensions observed.

These are strong assumptions. Even though we are not certain of the extent to which they are valid, it is useful nonetheless to undertake a preliminary but careful examination of recent changes in levels of apprehensions. One reason it is important to do so is that analyses of crude apprehensions statistics have been used to assess the impact of IRCA (Mathews, 1988; Suro, 1989). But although apprehensions data are useful for assessing changes in flows, their use must be tempered by caution born of an awareness of the assumptions involved.

In fact, border patrol apprehensions have declined since the passage of IRCA, from 1,609,278 in FY 1986 to 1,115,267 in FY 1987 and to 936,795 in FY 1988. As noted previously, however, the number of apprehensions of illegal aliens along the U.S.–Mexican border reflects in part the level and vigor of the INS effort to intercept the flow. For example, the number of hours devoted to patrolling the border has fluctuated over the years. To make apprehensions a better indicator of changes in the undocumented flow, the number of apprehensions must be freed of this important source of variation. A first step is to examine the number of apprehensions per hour of effort expended by the border patrol. Then changes in enforcement strategies that can influence apprehensions independently of the number of illegal crossings need to be taken into account. To minimize the influence of such changes, it is useful to focus attention on so-called line-watch apprehensions, which result from the direct patrolling of the border.

Table 6.1 includes data on the number of line-watch apprehensions, line-watch hours, and line-watch apprehensions per hour for fiscal years 1977–88. These years encompass three distinct periods. The first is 1977–82, a period of relative boom in the Mexican economy. During this time, line-watch apprehensions were relatively stable, or even declined slightly, at times, and the number of apprehensions per hour also declined slightly. The second period is 1983–86, after the collapse of the Mexican economy but before the passage of IRCA. During this time, line-watch apprehensions jumped sharply (by almost 46 percent from FY 1982 to FY 1983). After a lag, line-watch hours also increased. Most importantly, line-watch apprehensions per hour climbed substantially (by more than 47 percent compared to the 1977–82 years).

The third period includes 1987 and 1988, the two fiscal years after the passage of IRCA. During this time, apprehensions have declined, as have line-watch hours (again, after a lag) and, of chief importance, line-watch apprehensions per hour (see table 6.1). The degree of decline depends upon *which* pre-IRCA years are compared with *which* post-IRCA years, and upon whether total line-watch apprehensions or line-watch apprehensions per hour are used in the comparison.

Table 6.1 YEARLY LINE-WATCH APPREHENSIONS AND HOURS FY 1977–88

Fiscal Year	LWAs[a]	Line-Watch Hours	LWAs per Hour
1977	441,265	1,740,446	.254
1978	481,612	1,762,616	.273
1979	488,941	1,935,926	.253
1980	428,966	1,815,797	.236
1981	452,821	1,929,448	.235
1982	443,437	1,871,173	.237
1983	646,311	1,976,126	.327
1984	623,944	1,843,179	.339
1985	666,402	1,912,895	.348
1986	946,341	2,401,575	.394
1987	750,954	2,546,397	.295
1988	614,653	2,069,498	.297
	Mean	Mean	LWAs per Hour
1977–82	456,174	1,842,568	.248
1983–86	720,750	2,033,444	.354
1987–88	682,804	2,307,948	.296

a. LWAs, line-watch apprehensions.
Source: Unpublished tabulations by the United States Immigration and Naturalization Service.

For example, if one compares total line-watch apprehensions in post-IRCA 1988 only with those in 1986, one sees an approximate 35 percent decline. A comparison of the average number of apprehensions per line-watch hour for 1987 and 1988 with the average for 1983–86, however, shows a decline from 0.354 to 0.296 (see table 6.1), representing a decline of about 16 percent. Although this indicates only about half as much reduction as indicated by the 35 percent decline obtained by comparing only the gross number of apprehensions between 1986 and 1988, it nonetheless is a notable reduction. Whatever the basis of comparison, however, line-watch apprehensions have clearly not fallen to their 1977–82 levels. As to the extent to which IRCA has been responsible for any decline since 1986, one interpretation is that the legislation has stemmed only some of the increase in illegal crossings that appear to have resulted from the 1982 collapse of the Mexican economy, but it has not reduced illegal crossings to earlier levels (those of the 1977–82 period).

Any interpretation of such declines must also consider several other factors. First, FY 1986 appears to have been unique relative to the years that both preceded and followed it. Both enforcement and apprehension activities peaked in that one year. Until the reasons for this unique pattern are understood, pre-/post-IRCA comparisons using FY 1986 run the danger of overestimating effects attributable to IRCA.

Second, IRCA contains several provisions in addition to employer sanctions that can affect the value of the indicators, as already noted. For example, over 3 million newly legalized immigrants—more than 80 percent of whom are Mexican or Central American—no longer have to cross the border illegally for visits or for any other reason. This change alone could cause a decline in the number of illegal crossings, even if the number of first-time illegal crossings had not declined.

Third, the level and vigor of INS enforcement in areas other than the border will affect the value of the indicators in ways that have yet to be understood. As noted in chapter 4, enforcement at the interior has not yet been increased; enforcement of employer requirements has just begun; and only about 50 percent of employers are so far in full voluntary compliance.

Fourth, behavioral adjustments take time, and enough time may not have elapsed to expect a significant decline in illegal immigration. This is supported by a GAO (1987d) survey of eight countries that had implemented a similar law. In five of the eight, it took three to four years for employer sanctions to achieve a moderate or greater deterrent effect on illegal immigration.

Finally, factors unrelated to IRCA may also affect the value of these indicators. Foremost among those factors are changes in the demographic, political, and economic conditions of Mexico and Central America (Bean, Schmandt, and Weintraub, 1989). The growth in the population who are of labor-force age has outstripped growth in the number of new jobs in all countries of the Caribbean basin (Espenshade, 1989). Resulting pressures for out-migration can be further exacerbated (or decreased), depending on the political stability of sending countries. Similarly, U.S. changes in minimum wages, in foreign competition, or in the demand for labor can exercise an increased (or decreased) pull for illegal immigration.

To provide a quantitative assessment of the influence of these various factors, it is useful to rely on a number of different approaches. One would be to use apprehensions data disaggregated by sector and season to formally model the Mexican border-crossing process. Regression analysis and other statistical techniques could be employed to estimate the effects of relative wages, enforcement activities, season, and other factors on changes in the number of crossings. Parameter estimates would help to determine whether IRCA has led to changes in illegal flows coming to the United States. A decline in apprehensions might entirely reflect reduced illegal crossings by the legalized population, which can now cross the border legally. On the other hand, an increase in crossings does not necessarily signal the total ineffectiveness of IRCA provisions, but could reflect increased pressure to migrate in sending countries.

Another approach would be to look at changes in wages to test for changes in the supply of illegal immigrants. If the new law has been effective in decreasing the supply of illegal immigrants, wage rates in immigrant-dependent industries should rise—relative to compensation in other industries. Data on wage rates can be obtained from telephone surveys of entry-level wages offered by employers of dishwashers and janitors in major U.S. cities, some that are known as destinations for illegals, and some that are not.

Visas are another potential indicator of change in flows. Changes in the numbers of visas granted in countries that are traditionally large "suppliers" of illegal entrants who must enter the United States by air or sea can be monitored. A sharp drop in the number of visas or those countries would indicate that fewer people are attempting to come to the United States for illegal employment.

CONCLUSION

More definitive assessments of the extent to which IRCA has affected the stock and flow of illegal migrants to the United States will depend on an examination of many sources of data and indicators. For example, the number of line-watch apprehensions per unit of time is only one indicator, and one that applies primarily to flows from Mexico. It provides no information on the stock of Mexican illegals in the country. IRCA may also have the effect of reducing the *circulation* of labor migration from Mexico. If this were the case, flows (as measured by apprehensions, for instance) might be diminished, but the stock might be increased, other things being equal. This could happen if illegal migrants already in the country before IRCA but not eligible for legalization (a group some observers are calling the "residual" population) cut back sharply on the number of return trips to Mexico for fear of not being able to find a job when they circulate back to the United States. Also, apprehensions data provide little information about flows of illegal immigrants from countries other than Mexico, not to mention the stock of such persons.

In short, answering questions about the stock and flow of illegal immigrants depends upon fitting together a number of pieces of a puzzle. Much of the work suggested above is being carried out by the Program for Research on Immigration Policy. In addition, several other research efforts are likely to provide some of these pieces. The pioneering techniques of Robert Warren of the INS and Jeffrey S. Passel and Karen Woodrow at the Bureau of the Census on estimating the number of illegal migrants included in the 1980 Census and in Current Population Surveys are being applied to June 1988 CPS data and will yield a lower-bound estimate of the stock of illegals as of that date. Because of the size of the sample involved, however, the results of this research will be more meaningful for Mexican illegal migrants than for illegal migrants from other countries. Available evidence suggests that most of the latter are probably visa-overstayers. Robert Warren is currently preparing estimates of the number of overstayers in the country for periods both before and after IRCA. Douglas Massey of the University of Chicago is developing estimates of changes over time in the probability of an individual's undertaking a first illegal migration to the United States from Mexico. Other information, including data on school enrollments, hospital admissions, and the issuance of nonwage Social Security cards that show earnings histories, will be useful as well. All of these research projects will provide inputs to future efforts to assess whether IRCA has achieved its intended purpose of reducing illegal immigration to the United States.

Notes

1. This lag was even more pronounced in the case of *direct* as opposed to indirect examinations of the economic effects of undocumented immigration, most of which were published after IRCA was passed (Bean, Telles and Lowell, 1987; Bean, Lowell, and Taylor, 1988). Two recent studies that provide important indirect assessments of the effects of undocumented Mexican immigration on California were conducted by McCarthy and Valdez (1985) and Muller and Espenshade (1985).

2. In recent years, increasing numbers of illegal immigrants from Central American countries have also entered the country as EWIs.

Chapter Seven

LEGAL IMMIGRATION AND PROPOSED POLICY CHANGES

Just as the reality of and perceptions about continuing illegal immigration will undoubtedly affect whether IRCA is viewed as having accomplished its primary purpose, so too will perceptions about recent refugee flows and legal immigration influence policymakers' agendas about changes in legal immigration policy. Moreover, as noted earlier in this report, the question of whether or not IRCA has played a major role in bringing about major shifts in U.S. immigration policy, if indeed these shifts are occurring, requires an assessment of recent trends in legal immigration and policy. Hence, this chapter addresses three topics: (1) recent trends in refugee flows and asylee applications; (2) the recent pattern of legal immigration to this country; and (3) recent proposals that have emerged to modify U.S. legal immigration policy.

REFUGEE POLICY AND FLOWS

Chapter 6 emphasized the difficulty of ascertaining unequivocally whether IRCA has achieved some measure of success in deterring illegal immigration to the United States, although it has reduced aggregate illegal crossing at the Southern border. On the other hand, the number of legal entrants—refugees and legal immigrants—has been increasing.

Recent refugee flows are governed by the implementation of the provisions of the Refugee Act of 1980, which was designed to serve several purposes (Zucker and Zucker, 1987). First, the act attempted to reestablish congressional control over the number of refugees to be admitted every year—control that had been exercised since the 1950s largely by the executive branch in response to such immediate crises as the postrevolutionary exodus from Cuba. The annual limitation of refugee admissions was lifted from 17,400 (a number regularly exceeded before 1980 through the attorney general's authority to admit whole classes of refugees into the country) to a level whose annual limits would be generated through consultation between the president and Congress. The 1980 Refugee Act specifically forbid use of the attorney general's emergency admission power to admit refugees. In the act, Congress indicated that the annual level of refugee admissions would be expected to be 50,000, which represented the average annual admission of refugees to the United States from World War II to 1980. The 50,000 level has been exceeded by every annual consultation since 1980.

Second, the 1980 law removed ideological and geographical considerations from the definition of *refugee*, adopting instead the United Nations' more neutral standard of a "well-founded fear of persecution" as the statutory grounds for refugee status. Unlike previous policy that focused on communist-controlled countries, this standard was intended to apply equally to victims of all types of political oppression. The adoption of the internationally recognized definition of individual persecution was likewise intended to require individual, not mass or group, determination of refugee status.

Third, the Refugee Act gave statutory recognition to the principle of asylum. The petitions of both refugees and asylees would be evaluated on the basis of a uniform standard, i.e., whether the applicants had been subjected to a "well-founded fear of persecution" in their home countries. Asylees differ from refugees both in their method of petition and in the benefits to which they are entitled by U.S. law and policy. Refugees petition for entrance to the United States from outside U.S. borders. Once accepted for resettlement in the United States, they are entitled to apply for permanent residency status after one year (at which point, if their applications are approved, they are counted by the INS as legal immigrants in that year) and are granted access to a wide variety of social service benefits. Asylees, in contrast, first enter the United States, often without documentation, then petition the government for permission to remain. No preset limits exist for asylum applications. Those accepted for asylum may remain in the United States indefinitely in a "temporary" status and are permitted to work, but unlike refugees are not entitled to certain social service benefits. Up to 5,000 asylees may adjust to immigrant status each year.

Finally, the Refugee Act created the Office of Refugee Resettlement in the Department of Health and Human Services, through which federal policies regarding resettlement would be coordinated and implemented.

The extent to which foreign policy considerations have affected the conferral of refugee status and admission of refugees for settlement in the United States changed with the 1980 act. Congress, by adopting the United Nations (UN) definition and abandoning a definition limiting refugees to those fleeing countries with Communist governments, changed the criteria for refugee admissions. However, all who met the UN definition were not thereby eligible for admission to the United States. Their admission depended on their cases being of special humanitarian interest, a criterion whose spirit indicates less focus on foreign policy objectives, although such objectives are not wholly precluded by such a standard.

The Refugee Act itself emerged, in large measure, from a growing sense of responsibility in the United States for a coordinated evacuation of refugees from the communist governments of Southeast Asia. Indeed, from 1980 to 1982, Asian refugees constituted from 75 percent to 82 percent of refugee arrivals to the United States. Furthermore, their absolute numbers contributed to levels of refugee acceptance far exceeding the guideline of 50,000 refugees per year (see table 7.1).

An examination of table 7.1 suggests that foreign policy considerations continue to be reflected in refugee policy in the wake of the 1980 Refugee Act. The U.S. commitment to resettlement of postrevolutionary refugees from Asia is illustrated by the acceptance of over half a million Asian refugees from 1980 to 1986. Despite dramatic changes in regional political conditions, particularly in Latin America, the relative concentration of refugee admissions across regions remained fairly consistent from 1980 to 1988, with continued emphasis on Asia and the eastern Europe/Soviet Union regions—the source countries of U.S.-bound refugees before the 1980 law, when such determinations were made more explicitly on the basis of foreign policy. Indeed, the Reagan State Department's annual recommendations to Congress for refugee allocations repeatedly sought an expansion in the Soviet Union and Eastern Europe ceiling, while simultaneously suggesting reductions in Latin American admissions (Zucker and Zucker, 1987). By 1988, this pattern had emerged in the regional refugee allocations.

Refugee ceilings from Latin America (see table 7.1) declined steadily in the years of the Reagan administration, from over 20,000 in 1986 to 5,000, and eventually to a low of 1,000 in 1987. Actual arrivals

Table 7.1 U.S. REFUGEES BY REGION OF ORIGIN, FY 1980–88

	1980	1981	1982	1983[a]	1984	1985	1986	1987[b]	1988	Total[c]
AFRICA										
Ceiling	1,500	3,000	3,500	3,000	2,750	3,000	3,000	2,000	3,000	21,750
Actual arrivals	955	2,119	3,326	2,648	2,747	1,453	1,315	1,994	1,588	16,557
Percentage arrivals/ceiling	63.6	70.6	95.0	88.3	99.9	38.3	43.8	99.7	52.9	76.1
ASIA										
Ceiling	169,200	165,500	96,000	64,000	52,000	45,500	45,500	40,500	38,000	682,700
Actual arrivals	163,799	131,139	73,522	39,408	51,960	49,970	45,454	40,112	35,015	595,364
Percentage arrivals/ceiling	96.8	79.2	76.6	61.6	99.9	99.9	99.9	99.0	92.1	87.2
USSR										
Ceiling	33,000	33,000	20,000	15,000	11,000	10,000	9,500	12,300	30,000	87,800
Actual arrivals	28,444	13,444	2,756	1,409	715	640	787	3,698	20,421	27,670
Percentage arrivals/ceiling	86.2	40.7	13.8	9.4	6.5	6.4	8.4	30.0	68.1	31.5
EASTERN EUROPE										
Ceiling	5,000	6,900	11,000	—	—	—	—	—	—	87,800
Actual arrivals	5,025	6,704	10,780	12,083	10,285	9,350	8,713	8,606	7,818	56,855
Percentage arrivals/ceiling	100.5	97.2	98.0	80.5	93.5	93.5	96.8	70.0	26.1	64.7

LATIN AMERICA										
Ceiling	20,500	4,000	3,000	2,000	1,000	1,000	3,000	1,000	3,500	35,500
Actual arrivals	6,662	2,017	602	668	160	138	173	315	2,497	10,735
Percentage arrivals/ceiling	32.5	50.4	20.1	33.4	16.0	13.8	5.8	31.5	71.3	30.2
NEAR EAST SOUTH ASIA										
Ceiling	2,500	4,500	6,500	6,000	5,250	6,000	6,000	10,200	9,000	46,950
Actual arrivals	2,231	3,829	6,369	5,405	5,246	5,994	5,998	10,107	8,415	45,239
Percentage arrivals/ceiling	89.2	85.1	97.9	91.1	99.9	99.9	99.9	99.1	93.5	96.3
TOTAL										
Ceiling	231,700	217,000	140,000	90,000	72,000	70,000	67,000	70,000	83,500	957,700
Actual arrivals	207,116	159,252	97,355	61,681	71,113	68,045	62,440	64,828	75,754	791,830
Percentage arrivals/ceiling	89.4	73.4	69.5	68.5	98.8	97.2	93.2	92.6	90.7	82.7

Source: U.S. Department of State Bureau for Refugee; also cited in Zucker and Zucker (1987, p. 89).

a. After 1983, Eastern Europe ceiling is combined with USSR ceiling.

b. The 1987 total ceiling reflects an additional 4,000 admissions in the category, "Unallocated Reserve" for "contingent refugee admission needs," to be used only after consultation with Congress and only to the extent that private-sector funding is available to support those admissions.

c. For USSR and Eastern Europe since 1983, "Totals" equal combined ceiling and percentage.

peaked at 6,700 in 1980 and were as low as 173 in 1986. Overall since 1980, 30 percent of the authorized ceiling for Latin America has actually been used.

This discrepancy stems in part from the view that Latin American refugee petitioners are considered economic migrants. A longstanding history of Latin migration to the United States for economic reasons has established a precedent for the assumption that Latin American migrants are prompted to come to the United States as much by social networks and economic incentives as by the prospect of finding a haven from political persecution (U.S. Congress, 1984). Other factors influencing the U.S. government's approach to Latin American refugees have included the belief that Latin American refugees can find refuge in other Latin American countries and the fear that the proximity of Latin America to the United States could generate politically unacceptable levels of migration unless a firm and consistent stance is taken to discourage such flows. In keeping with these approaches, in 1986 the Reagan administration raised the ceiling from 1,000 to 3,000 for Latin American refugees, but named Cuba as the only country in Latin America qualifying as "a country of special humanitarian concern"—in effect, making Cubans the only Latin Americans eligible for refugee status under the Refugee Act. Partly as a result of this situation, many Latin Americans who might have petitioned for refugee status have turned to entering the United States and petitioning from within for political asylum.

The principle of asylum suggests that the receiving country evaluates the merit of every asylum application. In practice, the United States denies a large proportion of the asylum requests it adjudicates, with the denial rate varying substantially by country of origin. In FY 1987, 26 percent of the petitioners from Afghanistan, 67 percent from Iran, and 83 percent from Nicaragua were approved. At the same time, 4 percent of the petitioners from El Salvador and 4 percent of the Guatemalan petitioners were granted asylum (INS, 1987). While asylum cases are pending, the applicants are subject to the authority of the Department of Justice through the INS, meaning that they are under docket control and such benefits as travel and work authorization are made available at the discretion of the Department of Justice.

One of the major means implemented by the INS to deter asylum seekers—burden-of-proof requirements about persecution—was rejected in 1987 in the U.S. Supreme Court's decision *Cardoza-Fonseca v. INS*. The Court found that the INS had been requiring asylum seekers to provide a preponderance of evidence that they had been singled out individually for persecution—a standard considered more strict than that demanded in the Refugee Act of 1980. The Court found that the fear only had to be well-founded, not that there had to be a preponderance of evidence to indicate that persecution would be a likely outcome of the individual return. The effect of this decision remains to be seen.

The United States has further sought to deter asylum seekers from Central America by several means, including: selective detention practices; denial of due process protections to detained asylum seekers; and, in the case of Haitians, direct interdiction in international waters, followed by assisted and forced repatriation (Zucker and Zucker, 1987).

In 1981, prolonged detention periods imposed on Haitian asylum seekers in South Florida provoked charges that such incarceration violated the Fifth Amendment to the U.S. Constitution that no person shall be deprived of life, liberty, or property without due process of law, as well as the UN protocol banning unnecessary restrictions on movement of asylum seekers. Similar arguments emerged in 1988 with Central American asylum seekers in South Texas who were crossing the border in large numbers. The INS, believing many of the asylum claims to be frivolous, ordered asylum seekers to remain in South Texas until their applications were adjudicated, requiring thousands of Nicaraguans bound for Houston and Miami to remain in a rural area not equipped to accommodate large numbers of persons with limited resources for lengthy stays. A temporary restraining order imposed by a federal judge allowed the asylees to leave the Rio Grande Valley, but the issue remains unresolved and contentious. Denial of due process was found in the 1988 court decision *Orantes-Hernandez v. Smith,* in which a federal judge ordered the INS to cease coercive tactics imposed on detainees in efforts to pressure them to renounce their asylum claims.

The United States in 1981 adopted a policy of interdiction toward Haitian asylum seekers arriving by boat in Florida and entered into an agreement with the Duvalier government to intercept Haitian asylum seekers in international waters and repatriate them. INS officials were stationed on Coast Guard vessels patrolling southern waters. Haitian asylum seekers were interdicted, brought on board, adjudicated, and almost invariably returned to Haiti.

In spite of these practices, the number of asylum applicants, especially at certain entry points, remains high. From May to November of 1988, for example, the Harlingen, Texas INS district office, which covers the Rio Grande Valley, received 21,286 applications for political asylum. The applications for the entire year of 1987 at that office total only 405. Indeed, in November 1988, the INS received more applications in one day than the 1987 annual total for that location. October 1988 statistics on asylee countries of origin in the Harlingen district indicate that 54.2 percent were from Nicaragua, 19.9 percent from El Salvador, 11.6 percent from Honduras, 11.4 percent from Guatemala, and 2.9 percent from other nations ("Refugees Strain Valley INS Office," November 18, 1988). The total backlog in asylum adjudications nationwide reached 95,351 as of March 1988; taken together, the Cuban (74 percent), Nicaraguan (16 percent), Salvadoran (3 percent), and Haitian (1 percent) applications constituted 95 percent of the total applications pending (INS, 1988c).

Refugees and asylees are eligible to adjust their status to permanent legal residence after one year of U.S. residence. No annual numerical ceiling exists for refugee adjustments; but, as pointed out earlier in this chapter, asylee adjustments are restricted by the 1980 Refugee Act to 5,000 per year. Table 7.2 provides a summary of refugee and asylee status adjustments from 1980 to 1988.

In FY 1987, 91,474 refugees and in FY 1988, 105,276 refugees adjusted their status to permanent legal resident. The 1981–83 period reflects the high point thus far in the decade for refugee status adjustment, fueled largely by the population of refugees from the Viet-

Table 7.2 REFUGEE AND ASYLEE ADJUSTMENTS TO PERMANENT LEGAL RESIDENT STATUS, FY 1980–87

	Refugee Adjustments	Asylee Adjustments	Total Permanent Resident Aliens Admitted or Adjusted	Refugee and Asylee Adjustments as Percentage of Total
1980	74,585	1,250	530,639	14.3
1981	105,746	1,498	596,600	18.0
1982	154,742	1,859	594,131	26.4
1983	99,771	2,914	559,763	18.3
1984	86,520	5,607	543,903	16.9
1985	90,040	5,000	570,009	16.7
1986	99,383	5,000	601,708	17.3
1987	91,474	5,000	601,516	16.0
1988	105,276	5,445	643,025	17.2
TOTAL	907,537	33,573	5,241,294	18.0

Source: U.S. Immigration and Naturalization Service (INS), *1986 Statistical Yearbook of the Immigration and Naturalization Service*. Washington, D.C.: U.S. Department of Justice, 1987; and INS, *1987 Statistical Yearbook of the Immigration and Naturalization Service*. Washington, D.C.: U.S. Department of Justice, 1988.

nam era. In 1982, 77 percent of the adjustments were made by refugees from Vietnam, Laos, and Kampuchea (INS, 1983).

More recently, Cuba has emerged as the leading country of origin for refugees adjusting their status. In 1986 and 1987, Cuban refugees accounted for 30.5 percent and 29.4 percent, respectively, of total refugee adjustments (INS, 1988a). The pool of approximately 125,000 Marielitos influenced these numbers, because the Marielitos could adjust their status under prior legislation authorizing Cuban adjustments.

By the end of 1988 asylee adjustments had reached or surpassed the 5,000-person annual limit for the fifth consecutive year. In 1987, 60.9 percent of those adjusting from asylee status were from Iran. Nicaraguans represented 10.7 percent of the total. Poles represented 6.9 percent (INS, 1988).

Refugees and asylees have accounted for about 16 percent to 18 percent of all annual permanent legal resident admissions and adjustments since 1983 (see table 7.2). Asylee adjustments are expected to continue to reach the 5,000-person ceiling in the future (INS, 1988c). The number of refugee adjustments depends, in large measure, upon the number of refugee petitioners approved in previous years. Should new policies allow large numbers of refugees into the country at one time, as has been proposed for Soviet Jews seeking resettlement in the United States, the adjustment figures in the early 1990s will include these individuals, causing an upward spike (shorter or longer depending on Soviet exit policy and continued U.S. openness to Soviet exiles as refugees) in the proportion of refugees in the legal immigrant population.

RECENT PATTERNS OF LEGAL IMMIGRATION

By the end of FY 1988, the United States had averaged more than 552,000 legal immigrants per year during the 1980s. This level of immigration accounted for about 30 percent of the U.S. population growth during this period. Since 1985, legal immigration has exceeded 600,000 persons per year, reaching a high of 643,025 aliens granted permanent resident status in FY 1988 (INS, 1989). Almost all of the recent increase resulted from changes in the admission provisions as amended by IRCA. For example, IRCA amended the registry provision to allow persons residing continuously in the United

States since 1972 to qualify for immigrant status, and about 40,000 persons (three-fourths of whom were Mexican) adjusted under this provision.

The current policies with respect to legal immigration, adopted in 1965, and subsequently amended in 1976 and 1978, emphasize family unity as a major principle of immigration policy. Family ties to U.S. citizens or permanent resident aliens provide the basis for distributing 216,000 of the 270,000 U.S. visas available annually worldwide through the visa preference system. In FY 1987, 211,809 persons immigrated under the four family-based visa preference categories (INS, 1988a). In addition, several categories of family immigrants are exempt from the worldwide ceiling altogether: spouses of U.S. citizens, children of U.S. citizens, and parents of adult U.S. citizens. In FY 1987, 220,000 additional immigrants entered the United States via these exemptions (GAO, 1988a).

Family ties also serve as important factors in undocumented migration to the United States. For instance, the opportunity to enhance family income in the country of origin serves as an incentive for some family members to migrate to and work in the United States; and the presence of family members in the United States can reduce the direct and indirect costs of continued undocumented migration (Massey et al., 1987; Taylor, 1986).

Recent reform efforts indicate that some policymakers desire to separate family and labor-related criteria more sharply in immigration policy. For example, S.358, a bill introduced by Senators Edward Kennedy of Massachusetts and Alan Simpson of Wyoming that was approved by the Senate on July 13, 1989, would impose new limitations on visa eligibility for certain types of family members, reduce eligibility in one of the four family-based visa preference categories, and increase substantially the availability of visas based on labor-related characteristics. Also, the ineligible family members of the approximately 3 million undocumented immigrants who have applied to adjust their immigration status through IRCA's legalization programs would be eligible for "extended voluntary departure," meaning they could not be deported. They could apply for immigrant status under second preference as the spouse or child of a permanent resident alien, or wait until the legalized relative became a citizen (usually a minimum of five years after obtaining immigrant status) and then apply as an immediate relative of a U.S. citizen. Undocumented children would be eligible to legalize if both parents qualified for legalization under IRCA.

RECENT PROPOSALS TO CHANGE LEGAL
IMMIGRATION POLICY

The relative priority given to immigrants with family ties in the United States has come under increasing scrutiny in recent years, with pressures for changes continuing to mount in response to critics' charges about the policy's (1) fairness towards individuals without such ties in this country, resulting in a bias against immigration from Europe and Africa; and (2) incentives for ever-increasing levels of immigration as relatives qualify persons ever more distant from the original immigrant; and (3) inability to address the needs of the economy for skilled labor.

Two bills, the just-mentioned one sponsored by Senators Kennedy and Simpson and the other (H.R. 672) sponsored by Congressman Howard Berman of California and now being considered in the House, seek to address these issues in different ways. Table 7.3 compares the main provisions of these two bills to current policy.

The primary goals of the Kennedy-Simpson bill are to increase the proportion of legal immigrants admitted to the United States based on labor market needs rather than family relationships and to place a cap on overall legal immigration. An additional goal is to raise the low levels of northwestern European immigration; immigration from this area has decreased in the last two decades under the 1965 Immigration Act which abolished national origin quotas, while immigration from Latin America and Asia has increased dramatically.

There has been, of course, greater demand for visas to the United States from the developing countries of Asia and Latin America than from the more economically developed and stable European countries. This suggests the hypothesis that Asian and Latin American families may be more willing to split up in order for one family member to obtain permanent residency or citizenship status and then apply for visas for other family members. As a result both of such apparent national origin differences in behavior and of the change in 1965 to a more neutral national origins immigration policy, Latin Americans and Asians now account for approximately 80 percent of immigrants to the United States.

The Kennedy-Simpson bill attempts to modify immigration trends by creating two separate preference systems, one for family members and the other for "independent" immigrants. Under current law,

Table 7.3 PROPOSED LEGAL IMMIGRATION REFORM AS COMPARED TO CURRENT LAW

	Current Law	Kennedy-Simpson/Simon Compromise (S. 358)	Berman (H.R.672)
WORLDWIDE CAP	None	630,000 (for first three years)[a]	None
I. FAMILY IMMIGRATION:			
Nonpreference		480,000	
Immediate relatives, spouses, and children of adult U.S. citizens	Unlimited 220,000	Unlimited 220,000	Same as current law
Nonimmediate family preference system	270,000 ceiling	216,000 minimum level of total family preference visas	
First preference: unmarried adult sons and daughters of U.S. citizens	20% 54,000	9%[b] 24,200[c]	Same as current law
Second preference: spouses and unmarried sons and daughters of permanent residents	26% 70,200	57%[d] 148,000	Included in immediate relatives
Fourth preference: married sons and daughters of U.S. citizens	10% 27,000	9% 23,000	Same as current law
Fifth preference: brothers and sisters of adult U.S. citizens	24% 64,800	25% 64,800	Same as current law
II. INDEPENDENT IMMIGRATION:	Under nonimmigrant family ceiling of 270,000	150,000	150,000[e] 84,000 third and sixth preference/(employer sponsored) 66,000 (nonsponsored)
Special immigrants	Unlimited	2.7% 4,050	Same as current law
Rural medical personnel[f]	—	3.3% 4,950	—

Third preference: professionals and individuals of exceptional ability	10% 27,000	26.8%[g] 40,200	50% employer sponsored 42,000
Sixth preference: skilled or unskilled workers for which there is a need in U.S.	10% 27,000	26.8%[h] 40,200	50% 42,000
Employment-generating investors—$1 million in new capital, generate 10 jobs for U.S. citizens			
Retirees		4.5% 6,750	9% 5,940
Selected immigrants under point system[i]	—	—	15% 9,900
		any unused visas from the above categories	76% 66,000

MAXIMUM PER-COUNTRY VISA ALLOTMENT

	20,000	7%[j]	22,000

a. In the version of the bill passed by the Senate, this figure now represents a loose cap, since the number may be expanded to accommodate the 216,000 family preference visa minimum, depending on the level of immediate family immigration.

b. Any unused visas in one preference would be allocated to the next preference.

c. Kennedy-Simpson figures represent projections based on FY 1988 immigration levels.

d. Unmarried sons and daughters of permanent residents limited to under 26 years of age.

e. In Berman bill, total independent immigration is divided between employer-sponsored (third and sixth preferences) and nonsponsored (employment-generating investors, retirees, and selected immigrants).

f. Medical personnel must be state certified and work in a rural area for 10 years.

g. Professionals holding advanced degrees.

h. Kennedy-Simpson definition: Individuals capable of performing skilled labor not of a temporary or seasonal nature, for which a shortage of U.S. workers exists, and immigrants who hold baccalaureate degrees and are members of the professions.

i. Any unused visas in the Kennedy-Simpson independent immigration system are allocated to "selected immigrants" category.

j. Maximum per-country visa allotment in S.358: 7% for family-related immigration; 7% for independent immigration.

independent immigrants, or individuals immigrating on the basis of their occupational skills, apply in the third and sixth categories of the preference system and are allotted 20 percent of the current 270,000 ceiling. The proposed bill would create separate avenues of entrance for immigrants with needed skills, and would more than double the number of visas available on the basis of skills from 54,000 to 150,000.

The bill also sought to establish, for the first time in U.S. history, a cap on overall immigration. The total number of visas issued per year would be 630,000, with 480,000 of these allocated to immigrants with family ties in the U.S. and 150,000 to independent immigrants. There would be a 7 percent country limit for each of the two systems. However, in a major departure from previous practice, the bill requires the president to review the appropriateness of these numerical ceilings every three years and recommend changes if warranted.

Also under the proposed bill, family preference visas, excluding immediate relatives of U.S. citizens, would be distributed according to the following preference system:

□ Unmarried adult sons and daughters of U.S. citizens—9 percent (first preference)
□ Spouses and unmarried sons and daughters under age 26 of legal permanent residents—57 percent (second preference)
□ Married sons and daughters of U.S. citizens—9 percent (fourth preference)
□ Brothers and sisters of adult U.S. citizens—25 percent (fifth preference)

Any unused visas in one preference would be allocated to the next preference.

This preference system differs from the existing system in several important ways. Currently, the number of visas for immediate relatives of U.S. citizens (spouses, minor children, and parents) is unlimited and is independent of the family preference system. The proposed bill, while keeping the number of visas for immediate relatives of U.S. citizens unlimited, would base the number of available family preference visas on the level of immediate relative immigration. The number admitted under the family preference categories would be limited to 480,000 minus the number of immediate relatives of U.S. citizens admitted in the previous fiscal year. Thus, any increase in the immediate relative category would reduce accordingly the number of available family preference visas. However, the bill was amended on the Senate floor to guarantee a minimum of 216,000 family preference visas (the 1988 level) regardless of how many immediate relatives of citizens had entered the previous year. The ceiling, as Senator Simpson remarked, has a hole in it.

Nearly 220,000 individuals entered in FY 1987 as immediate family members of U.S. citizens. If this number did not increase, it would leave 260,000 available visas (480,000 minus 220,000) for nonimmediate relatives of citizens and immediate family members of aliens compared to the 216,000 who entered in 1988. However, the number of immediate relative applications has been increasing year by year. As this trend is expected to continue, it will lead to a decrease in the availability of visas for nonimmediate relatives of citizens and legal aliens' nuclear families. Despite the 216,000 minimum level of family preference visas, the proposed nonimmediate ceilings may eventually result in increased backlogs due to demand for the limited visas.

In the second preference under current law, there is no age limit on eligible unmarried children of permanent residents. S.358 would limit the second preference to unmarried children of permanent residents under the age of 26. Proponents of S.358 argue that this change will actually increase immigration for this category, despite the new age limit, because S.358 allocates an increase in the number of second preference visas. Critics argue, however, that Kennedy-Simpson would decrease the availability of second preference visas over time. They anticipate that the demands for second preference visas will outnumber the supply, in spite of the additional allocations. Moreover, they predict that this increased demand would be the direct result of recently passed and proposed immigration reforms, arising from requests from the immediate family members of permanent residents who legalized under IRCA and families of labor track immigrants, who, under the Kennedy-Simpson bill would not be allowed to bring their families with them.

Under the Kennedy-Simpson proposal, economic criteria and professional skills would be more important in the choice of immigrants. Up to 150,000 visas would be available annually to "independent" immigrants. The separate system of independent visas would be distributed according to the following system:

☐ Special immigrants (for example, ministers of religion, former employees of U.S. embassies, etc.)—2.7 percent.
☐ Rural medical personnel—these individuals must be state certified

and must work in a rural area of the United States for 10 years—3.3 percent.

☐ Professionals with advanced degrees or individuals of exceptional ability in the sciences, arts, or business—26.8 percent (third preference).

☐ Workers with skills for which there is a shortage in the United States and professionals with bachelor's degrees—26.8 percent (sixth preference).

☐ Employment-generating investors, who must invest $1 million in a commercial enterprise benefiting the U.S. economy and creating employment for 10 U.S. citizens or legal permanent residents—4.5 percent.

☐ Selected immigrants, who must score 60 points out of a total of 90 in a point system based on level of education, occupation, occupational training or work experience, and prearranged employment. Of these visas, 18.5 percent are reserved for people from the 36 "disadvantaged" countries (immigration from these countries became more difficult after the 1965 amendments to the Immigration and Nationality Act as determined by the State Department). The first 20 percent of the visas go to those individuals with the highest number of points—whatever proportion results from this category plus any unused visas in the previously mentioned categories.

The categories of rural medical personnel, employment-generating investors and selected immigrants are new and aimed at attracting better-educated and skilled workers. Under current law, unskilled workers are included in the sixth preference category, but in the proposed system they are excluded completely. Also, existing law does not require an individual to have a bachelor's degree when applying as a professional or skilled worker. Finally, the selected immigrants are the only ones, in both the independent and the family systems, who cannot bring their spouses and children with them under the same category. The family must join the immigrant later, either as a second preference applicant under the family preference system, (which could add to the backlog previously discussed), or, if an immigrant applicant becomes a citizen, as the immediate family member of a U.S. citizen. In either case, the family members may be separated for years.

The current Kennedy-Simpson bill is similar to a bill that passed the Senate in 1988 but was not voted on in the House of Representatives. It reflects certain changes made as a compromise to a bill introduced by Senator Paul Simon, legislation which has since been dropped.

Simon's bill contained no overall ceiling on immigration and did not link immediate family immigration to nonimmediate family immigration. It also provided for a larger number of family preference visas than are available under current law. The original Kennedy-Simpson bill cut back substantially the number of visas available in the fifth preference, the backlogged category of brothers and sisters of adult U.S. citizens, and limited that category to never-married brothers and sisters.

The compromise bill contains a cap on overall immigration but retains the fifth preference as it is in current law. In addition, the bill as it currently stands does not include English language as a criterion in the point system for selected immigrants, as was included in the original Kennedy-Simpson version.

Other changes to the original bill include an amendment to end direct federal benefits, including Social Security, to undocumented immigrants and a provision to grant stays of deportation to immediate relatives of individuals legalizing under IRCA. The bill also includes an amendment to exclude undocumented immigrants in the Census Bureau's official population counts used for legislative apportionment. Also, in response to the repression of prodemocracy demonstrators in China, the bill provides for an increase in the annual immigration level for Hong Kong from 2 percent to 3.5 percent of the worldwide total. It also allows Chinese students to remain in the United States for four years and to qualify for legal residency.

Pending in the House of Representatives is the bill sponsored by Congressman Berman, which is essentially a companion to the pre-compromise Simon bill in the Senate. The only significant difference between the two is Berman's provision to make immediate relatives of permanent residents exempt from the existing family preference limit, treating them like immediate relatives of U.S. citizens (see table 7.3 for a comparison).

The Kennedy-Simpson bill as passed by the Senate includes no provisions for beneficiaries of the IRCA legalization program to speed the process of obtaining visas. It does provide, as mentioned, that they may not be deported if apprehended in the United States while still undocumented. Within the next year, 2 million to 3 million individuals could potentially earn permanent resident status and thus be able to seek visas for their spouses and children under the current second preference. In five more years, these permanent residents will be eligible to apply for citizenship, and many of them may attempt to sponsor spouses or children as immigrants (if they have so far been unable to get them into the United States due to long backlogs in the second preference) as well as their parents, whose entry they could sponsor as immediate relatives of United States citizens. This could lead to an increase in immediate relative immigration that could curtail availability of visas for nonimmediate families of citizens and immigrants' spouses and children. Although 216,000 of these visas are guaranteed under the Kennedy-Simpson bill, the demand for them is also expected to increase.

In conclusion, the Kennedy-Simpson and Berman bills would increase the total number of available immigrant visas and facilitate the immigration of professionals and skilled workers. However, it is not clear if the bills would achieve the goal of increasing the proportion of immigrants from northwestern European countries. Neither do the bills address the problem of existing backlogs, nor do they address the important issue of an inevitable surge in the number of permanent residents, and eventually of naturalized citizens, resulting from IRCA's legalization programs. These persons will bring increased demand for both immediate family and family preference visas. However, both bills would set in motion a periodic review of the number of legal immigrants, leaving the door open for adjustments in future years.

Chapter Eight

CONCLUSIONS AND A LOOK
TO THE FUTURE

IRCA is without question a complex and potentially far-reaching piece of legislation. It arose amidst many concerns, among the more important of which were the following: that illegal immigration was too high and harmful to the country, that it was important to preserve the nation's generous policies toward legal immigration, that efforts to eliminate the existing illegal population in the country should follow paths that would extend civil and constitutional rights to the members of this population, that legislation should not be enacted that did not include safeguards to prevent employment discrimination against authorized workers, and that the labor needs of agricultural employers needed to be taken into consideration. The provisions implemented as a reflection of these concerns are now close to three years old. Sufficient time has passed for some early effects of the legislation to be discerned. But it is still unclear whether the passage of IRCA represents the beginning of a new era in U.S. immigration policy.

One of IRCA's major objectives is to curtail illegal immigration to the country. The examination of apprehensions data collected at the Mexican border yields results that appear consistent with the possibility that some dampening effect on illegal crossings may have occurred, although one that may owe in part to IRCA's legalization programs. Other sources of information and data than apprehensions statistics, however, must be examined before firmer conclusions can be reached about the extent to which IRCA may have altered illegal migration flows from Mexico to the United States as opposed to having only reduced the circulation of persons already residing in the country. In the long term, the effectiveness of IRCA will depend upon both the level and the sustenance over time in INS interdiction activities at the border and INS enforcement of employer sanctions.

Whatever the final verdict about IRCA's effectiveness in reducing illegal flows, the legislation represents an important and tangible first step towards redefining U.S. immigration policies. Further changes may be forthcoming. The Kennedy-Simpson bill, recently passed in the Senate, and its counterpart, introduced by Berman in the House, together constitute another step in the direction of reforming the U.S. legal immigration policies. Although the two bills differ on the significant issue of whether immediate relatives of immigrants are to be allowed to enter the country without limitation, they pull in the same direction on many other issues: anticipation of increases in the total number of legal immigrants at levels above the peak levels of the 1980s; the need to increase the number of immigrants admitted for labor market/economic conditions; the need to open more widely the opportunities for would-be immigrants without family ties here; and the need to periodically revise numerical ceilings placed on the number of legal immigrants admitted to the country.

In regard to the issue of whether the United States appears to be moving toward a new era in its immigration policies, we do not feel the evidence is clear enough to answer this question. IRCA's significance in this regard is not clear-cut, since its provisions may ultimately be interpreted as either restrictionist or nonrestrictionist. IRCA's eventual impact will be clarified only in relation to continuing immigration trends and policy developments that will have a bearing on how the act is viewed, and even these may not prove decisive. For example, the Kennedy-Simpson bill, might be viewed as nonrestrictionist or even expansionist in its provision for currently rather high levels of or even increases in legal immigration. On the other hand, it might be viewed as potentially restrictionist in that it places a cap, albeit a loose one, on legal immigration. Whatever interpretation eventually is given to U.S. immigration trends and policies of the 1980s, it is likely that they will be shaped by many forces, including not only the immigration patterns and policies themselves but numerous other factors affecting the country. The remainder of this report speculates about some of the conditions that may affect immigration trends and the policy reactions to them, as well as about some of the research issues that need to be investigated to help formulate further changes in immigration policy.

IRCA's final implementation has yet to be fully felt—especially the institutionalization of its new hiring and antidiscrimination policies, which affect all Americans, and the unfolding of other secondary processes which result from the newly legalized population sponsoring family members as immigrants. The size of recent and foreseeable immigration—including the approximately 3 million persons legalized by IRCA and the role of refugees in recent flows and apparent continued demand for refugee admissions—as well as the change in contemporary migration from European to Asian and Latin origins—all are likely to make strong demands on American institutions, society, and culture. Current and anticipated immigration patterns may spell change, more rapid and deeper, than we have known since the heyday of immigration around the turn of the century.

In the early 1900s, Americans became more and more aware of the closing of the frontier, of the replacement of an agrarian economy by an industrial economic base, and of a trend toward urbanism and away from a rural or small-town way of life. There was recognition that important changes were under way in America and that the new immigrants arriving in great numbers from southern and eastern Europe hastened the change, directed it, and gave it a texture it would otherwise not have had.

Today, at the end of the 1980s, the country is in a "postindustrial," "postmodern" era. With the economy increasingly international in scope, calls are frequently heard to restructure the nation's industrial base and to develop an information/communication-based economy. As in the past, concern over social and economic changes includes an element of uneasiness about America's capacity to compete and prosper and, more pointedly, about the nation's ability to maintain an identity and continuity with our past. Immigration is a reflection of and a contributor to some, but by no means all, of these changes. Nor is immigration always the most important source of change. Trade deficits, for example, appear to lead to more wage reduction and job displacement in the U.S. labor force than does immigration (Freeman, 1988). This finding is consistent with research that has revealed that legal and illegal immigration have only small (and sometimes positive) effects on the wages and employment of native workers (for example, Bean, Telles, and Lowell, 1987; Borjas and Tienda, 1987). Nevertheless, immigrants do appear to exert a negative effect on the labor market prospects of other immigrants, thus underscoring the need to develop sound immigrant policies, i.e., policies that promote the social and economic integration of immigrants once they have come to this country.

In general, then, there is a need to define the role of immigration and the integration of immigrants within American society. Areas of American life where immigrants are most likely to exert effects warrant monitoring, including: the economy (for example, the operation of the job market—who is hired and fired, who fills what jobs, and how rewards are distributed ethnically); education (the fundamental pathway to economic advancement, which is itself also affected by immigrants); religion and religious institutions (for example, what is the effect of immigration on religious denominations and church membership? and how does immigration influence Roman Catholicism, mainline Protestant churches, evangelical and fundamentalist Christian churches, and Jewish identification and religious membership?); political institutions (for example, what are the patterns of political affiliation and identification of the new immigrant groups? The defection of some European ethnic groups from President Franklin Roosevelt's coalition to Republicanism suggests that immigrant groups do not necessarily and uniformly become Democrats).

In conclusion, the institutional life of America (its schools, religious denominations, political parties); its culture as portrayed in the arts, literature, music, television, sports, and movies, the ingredients of which help to define our national identity; and the economy as reflected in the job market—all merit study for the ways in which they are shaped by immigration and vice versa. Some parts of our lives will no doubt be found to be more affected than others, just as some regions of the country will feel the effects of immigration and policy changes more than others. The broad sweep of IRCA on immigration, jobs, civil rights, and federal reimbursement of state and local governments in itself is a measure of the perception that immigration widely affects us. Not only should we continue to monitor IRCA, but we should continue to assess the process, as old as America itself, that led legislators to adopt IRCA.

America is still a nation of immigrants, and as a people, we are still ambivalent about this reality. IRCA is neither the beginning nor the end of social change but a moment, in fact a measure, of reaction to what was perceived as sizable immigration from new sources, on a scale that still continues. Even as we focus on IRCA's details, describe its implementation, and attempt to measure its impacts, IRCA is but part of a larger process. Immigration on a large scale continues as an integral part of the American experiment. Temporary worker programs, refugee resettlements, and the abandonment of national-origins-dominated admissions criteria have helped to maintain and reinvigorate immigration from the lows it experienced in the 1930s and early 1940s. Today, as yesterday, two main questions will continue to dominate the ongoing debate: (1) what are we to do about—how do we react to—the large and changing immigration of the last quarter century and more? and (2) should the country curtail future immigration, either near its current level, at a higher level or at a reduced level of admission?

These questions not only should guide future policy research dealing with immigration, they will also frame the alternative policy responses available to the country. The particular responses selected will, in part, reflect the perceptions and realities of the effects of the continuing growth in cultural, linguistic, and economic diversity on American institutions and Americans' understanding of themselves. Whether a cap is imposed on immigration; whether family reunification is deemphasized in favor of criteria focusing on job-related skills; whether the focus of immigration moves from family criteria to economic criteria; and whether programs are adopted to facilitate the social integration and economic advancement of immigrants are all important policy issues. Their resolution will reveal the nature and direction of the country's evolving immigration policies.

APPENDICES

A SUMMARY OF IRCA RELATED ACTIVITIES, NOVEMBER 1986 TO FEBRUARY 1989

LEGALIZATION PROGRAMS
LAW Program
 Number of applications filed[a]   1.77 million
  Number of temporary residence granted[a] 1.31 million
  Approval rate (percent)[a] 97.8
  Number of pending applications 0.43 million
 Number of applicants for permanent residence[b] 78,202
  Number of permanent residence granted 22,393
  Approval rate (percent) 99.8
  Number of pending applications 55,805
Special Agricultural Workers Program (SAWs)
 Number of applications filed 1.31 million
  Number of temporary residence granted[a] 0.33 million
  Approval rate (percent)[a] 93.9
  Number of pending applications[a] 0.96 million
 Number of applicants for permanent residence NA[c]

EMPLOYER EDUCATION
 Number of handbooks distributed by INS[d] 10.74 million
 Number of employer contracts by INS[d] 1.80 million

ENFORCEMENT OF EMPLOYER REQUIREMENTS
INS[d]
 Number of employers investigated 15,387
  Targeted[e] 11,753
  Random[e] 3,634
 Number of employers cited or warned 3,683
 Number of intents to fine 1,387
  Amount of "intents to fine" (in $ millions) 6.00
 Number of final orders 610
  Amount of final orders (in $ millions) 1.00
  Amount collected to date (in $ millions) 0.56
 Number of hearings requested NA[f]
  Number of hearings completed 3
  Number in which INS was sustained 2
DOL

Number of I–9 audits made[g]	49,809
BORDER PATROL ENFORCEMENT	
Number of border patrol agents in the field (FY 1988)[h]	3,719
Line-watch hours (in full-time staff equivalent)[i] (FY 1988)	1,061
Number of aliens apprehended (FY 1988)	969,000
INTERIOR ENFORCEMENT	
Number of deportable aliens apprehended (FY 1988)	37,026
ENFORCEMENT OF ANTIDISCRIMINATION PROVISIONS	
Office of Special Counsel on Employment Discrimination (OSC, Department of Justice)[j]	
Number of discrimination charges received	454
Number of discrimination charges disposed of[k]	259
Number settled[l]	56
Number of charges filed with Administrative Law Judge[m]	40
Number disposed of[n]	11
AGRICULTURAL SPECIAL PROVISIONS	
H–2A Program[o]	
Number of requests submitted to DOL	22,102
Approval rate (percent)	80%
Number of jobs certified	19,939
INS BUDGET (in $ thousands)	
Total expenditures FY 1988	1,024,356
FY 1988 revenues from fees	216,597
FY 1989 budget	1,038,500

Sources: U.S. Immigration and Naturalization Service; U.S. Department of Labor; Office of Special Counsel on Employment Discrimination, U.S. Department of Justice; presidential budget, FY 1990.

a. As of January 27, 1989.

b. As of February 20, 1989. Holders of the temporary residence status must apply for permanent residence during a time window beginning 18 months after receipt of their temporary residence and ending 30 months thereafter.

c. Not applicable. SAWs participants will be eligible for permanent residence beginning in December 1989.

d. As of January 1989. Employer contacts include mailings and face-to-face visits.

e. "Targeted" includes investigations resulting from local information available such as complaints, FBI tips, suspicion that certain industries hire undocumented workers, records of past violations, and referrals from DOL I–9 audits. "Random" includes investigations initiated by random selections of firms. Random selection is done centrally at INS headquarters in Washington, D.C.

f. NA, not available.

g. As of January 31, 1989.

h. As of the end of FY 1988. Excludes 435 agents in training and 765 agents performing managerial, training, and other functions.

i. Based on 478,922 reported line-watch hours divided by 1,950 hours per full-time employee. Line-watch hours measure resources allocated to border interdiction activities.

j. As of February 20, 1989.

k. Includes cases closed because of lack of jurisdiction, withdrawal by charging parties, no discrimination was found, insufficient evidence, or a settlement was reached.

l. Most of the settled cases were in favor of the employee (i.e., plaintiff). The remaining 78 percent of cases disposed of were either dismissed because of negative determination and/or no reasonable cause discrimination occurred or lack of jurisdiction (70 percent); or did not have enough evidence to prosecute (8 percent).

m. Eleven were filed by the OSC and the other 29 directly by the plaintiff or by an organization on behalf of the plaintiff.

n. Most (9) were settled prior to trial.

o. For July 1987 to June 1988. See DOL (1988).

THE PROGRAM FOR RESEARCH ON IMMIGRATION POLICY:
Research Mission and Initial Public Policy Agenda

I. GOALS OF THE PROGRAM

With funding from The Ford Foundation, The RAND Corporation and The Urban Institute jointly established the Program for Research on Immigration Policy in February 1988. Aimed at providing analysis that will help inform immigration and immigrant policies,[1] the Program has three basic goals:

☐ To study the important domestic and international issues raised by the Immigration Reform and Control Act (IRCA) of 1986,
☐ To address the larger continuing questions and problems of immigration and immigrant policies, and
☐ To disseminate and exchange information about IRCA and immigration through publications, working groups, and conferences.

During the Program's first two years, it is concentrating its research agenda on IRCA and its effects. In subsequent years, it will widen its field to studying larger issues involving immigration and immigrant policies.

As a nationally respected, nonpartisan research center on immigration, the Program will contribute to the understanding of IRCA in particular and of immigration and immigrant policies in general. It will also disseminate findings to help reform current immigration laws and inform future ones.

Objective, nonpartisan research on IRCA and its effects is essential for future deliberations concerning U.S. immigration policies. Such research will provide information to determine whether and how much the new law is failing to achieve its objectives and the reasons for this failure. Among other things, such research will inform decisions over the possible "sunsetting" of IRCA's employer sanctions when Congress reviews them in late 1989 and early 1990. In addition, it will inform important policy decisions that the law assigns to IRCA's administering agencies, including enforcement targeting strategies and the need for support services to the population that has received amnesty.

Beyond this, research will help policymakers identify and, where needed, correct potentially undesirable outcomes of IRCA. It should also help practitioners assess the effectiveness of the several untested "tools" of immigration policy, including IRCA's legalization, employer requirements, and employer sanctions. Finally, research will help assess the extent to which IRCA's success or failure results from its design or from its implementation.

II. OVERVIEW OF THE PROGRAM
FOR RESEARCH ON IMMIGRATION POLICY

To provide this needed research, the Program for Research on Immigration Policy has devised an initial set of eight complementary research activities grouped under three major headings:

IRCA's Implementation

1. General provisions
2. Special agricultural provisions

IRCA'S Domestic Effects

3. Illegal immigrants coming to the United States
4. The U.S. economy in general
5. U.S. agriculture in particular
6. Illegal immigrants remaining in the United States

IRCA'S International Effects

7. U.S.–Mexican relations
8. Sending countries

With the exception of Projects 4 and 8, these research activities have already begun.

IRCA'S IMPLEMENTATION

IRCA is a complex piece of legislation with implementation strategies that potentially affect every individual, every federal, state, and local institution, and nearly every private and nonprofit firm in the country. Implementation of its more than 50 provisions is being staggered over the five-year period that began in November 1986.

The following two research projects aim at identifying and explaining differences between policymakers' intentions and government actions, identifying the incentives for and costs of compliance, and projecting IRCA's likely effects. Together, these two projects will provide the basis for judging whether IRCA's eventual success or failure can be ascribed to its design or implementation.

1. Implementation of IRCA's General Provisions

The first project aims at assessing how and how fully IRCA's policies are implemented and how they affect the behavior of immigrants, employers, government agencies, and service providers. The project's unique design focuses on the interactions and cumulative (and potentially conflicting) effects of the various provisions of IRCA, tracking changes over time. These provisions include legalization and amnesty, employer requirements and sanctions, antidiscrimination provisions, grants to states, and entitlement verification. The project is also examining the interactions among federal, state, and local government agencies and voluntary organizations. Because the law was enacted by a diverse coalition of interest groups with different goals, the project takes into account political factors at all three levels of government. To do so, it is examining eight localities that represent the full range of immigrant groups and INS regions:

□ Texas: El Paso, Houston, and San Antonio;
□ California: Los Angeles and San Jose;
□ East Coast: New York and Miami;
□ Midwest: Chicago

Together, these localities contain 85 percent of the undocumented population that applied for amnesty.

2. Implementation of IRCA's Special Agricultural Provisions

IRCA has three special provisions aimed at assuring that the agricultural industry will have an adequate labor supply:

☐ The Special Agricultural Worker (SAW) Program, which extends amnesty to agricultural workers who have worked 90 days in U.S. agriculture between May 1985 and May 1986,
☐ the Replenishment Agricultural Worker (RAW) Program, which provides for the legal and eventually permanent entry of additional workers for agriculture outside the ceilings for legal immigration, and
☐ a streamlined H–2A Program, which permits wider use of foreign temporary labor when labor shortages can be demonstrated.

This second project is assessing how and to what extent these three special provisions are put into effect, how they interact with IRCA's other provisions, how they affect the behavior of individual farmers, and how they affect sectors other than agriculture. Initially, this project is paying special attention to SAW's provisions, which place the burden of proof on the INS to establish that aliens are not eligible for amnesty. (This is an exception to IRCA's general provisions, which place the burden of proof on aliens to establish that they are eligible for amnesty.) In addition, workers admitted into the country under the SAW Program can subsequently shift from agricultural jobs to other types of employment. As a consequence, this project is investigating the movement of SAW workers from rural to urban areas.

IRCA'S DOMESTIC EFFECTS

IRCA aims at stemming the tide of illegal immigrants coming to and remaining in the United States primarily by removing their economic incentive to do so. In making it illegal for employers to hire undocumented workers, the law seeks to reduce the demand for their services. Relying on enhanced enforcement by INS border patrols and inspectors, the law is expected to benefit some groups of the labor force without unduly harming the U.S. economy in general or U.S. agriculture in particular.

The following projects address key questions regarding the domestic effects of IRCA. They investigate the effects on illegal immigrants coming to the United States, on the distribution of costs and benefits in the labor force, and on the economy—especially in regions and industries that have traditionally depended on undocumented labor. Although the framers of the law expected that undocumented aliens not eligible for amnesty would eventually leave the country, concern has been growing about the development of a permanent underclass open to economic and social exploitation in the event this expectation is not realized. Our last project explores this important and difficult question.

3. IRCA's Effects on Illegal Immigrants Coming to the United States

This project is assessing changes in the flow of immigrants who cross the border illegally or who overstay the duration of their visas. Because flows of illegal immigrants cannot be observed directly, this project is measuring changes over time in several direct and indirect demographic, administrative, and economic factors. Also, it seeks to discover how "coyotes" (professionals who bring illegal immigrants across the border) perceive IRCA's effects on illegal immigration. To determine how IRCA affects the stocks of illegal immigrants remaining in the country, the project is working with officials in the United States Bureau of the Census and researchers at the INS.

4. IRCA's Effects on the U.S. Economy in General

IRCA is expected to change the supply and demand not only for low-wage undocumented workers but also for newly legalized ones. In turn, these changes should alter:

□ Labor market opportunities of other labor groups, such as low-skilled native workers, other legal immigrants, and native-born ethnic workers, and
□ the competitive position of particular sectors of the economy (such as the garment and electronics industries) and particular regions of the country (such as California and Texas) that previously depended on undocumented workers.

Not yet underway, this project will identify and measure the direction and size of these changes. If IRCA is ineffective in reducing the numbers of illegal workers entering the country, this project will also consider how an effective law would influence the U.S. economy.

5. IRCA's Effects on U.S. Agriculture in Particular

In the past, U.S. agriculture depended heavily on both legal and illegal immigrants for its supply of labor. If successful, IRCA will reduce the net supply of workers legalized through the SAW Program. This project is identifying IRCA's influence on:

□ Farm labor and wages, and
□ individual farmers' employment practices, production decisions, and adoption of new labor-saving technologies.

In addition, this project is examining whether differential effects are occurring on various crops, labor activities, and agricultural regions.

6. IRCA's Effects on Illegal Immigrants Remaining in the United States

About three million previously undocumented aliens are in the process of being legalized under IRCA's amnesty provisions. However, some who are eligible for amnesty may not have applied, and many undocumented aliens remain ineligible. How many remain or will remain in the country is unknown. This raises concerns about IRCA's overall effects, especially that it may create a new "underclass" that is highly vulnerable to exploitation. Job opportunities for undocumented workers may narrow increasingly through enforcement of IRCA's prohibitions on hiring them. As a consequence, self-employment among the undocumented may increase. No population-based surveys of illegal residents have been previously conducted because it is difficult and costly to distinguish illegal immigrants not only from legal immigrants but also from the native population. To survey illegal and legal immigrants, this project is developing and testing methods for representative sampling of these populations. It will provide preliminary descriptive information on their comparative experiences both before and after IRCA and on the ways that IRCA affects their behavior and job opportunities. In addition, this representative sampling should provide the basis not only for estimating the number of undocumented illegals who remain in the country but also for developing longitudinal surveys concerning immigrants' economic opportunities and cultural adjustments to the United States.

IRCA's INTERNATIONAL EFFECTS

IRCA will affect not merely the United States but also those countries that have traditionally sent illegal immigrants to the United States. In addition, actions and considerations in "sending" countries may affect the character of IRCA's implementation as well as the nature and magnitude of its effects in the United States. In turn, IRCA's implementation in the United States and responses to it in sending

countries may affect international relations, the economic and political stability of some sending countries, and their domestic policies
and institutions. The two projects outlined below take a first step
toward addressing these important interrelationships.

7. IRCA's Effects on U.S.–Mexican Relations

No sending country is more affected by IRCA than Mexico. Mexicans
account for 55 to 65 percent of the estimated illegal population residing here, and U.S. immigration policies are a continuing source
of controversy and tension between the two countries. This project
aims at discovering the views of selected Mexican and U.S. authorities concerning

☐ IRCA's effects on both countries and their relations, and
☐ the effects of immigration-related issues on future U.S. and Mexican policies dealing with each other.

This project emphasizes two themes: changes in the public dialogue
concerning immigration policy in both countries and changes in
Mexico's views of regional development and the borderlands. The
United States has often claimed that it should close its border to
Mexican immigrants but that Mexico should open its borders to
American investment. Mexico has claimed the exact opposite. IRCA
may influence a change in these attitudes.

8. IRCA's Effects on Sending Countries

In the past decade, the United States became an increasingly important source of permanent and temporary employment for immigrants from several Central American and Caribbean countries (such
as El Salvador and the Dominican Republic) and several Asian countries (such as the Philippines and Korea). Through remittances made
to relatives in the home countries, immigrant workers appear to have
made substantial contributions to their home country's balance of
payments, local businesses, and economic development. These immigrant workers also have contributed to the direct economic and
social well-being of their families. Not yet underway, this project
will determine how much IRCA is influencing these effects, including foreign domestic institutions and policies involving regional investments. In the case of Mexico, this project will also assess the
effects of establishing a Mexican commission that would parallel

IRCA's U.S. Commission for the Study of International Migration and Cooperative Economic Development.

In sum, these research projects should make a major contribution to documenting and understanding the implementation and effects of this major new immigration policy. Taken together, their findings will assist in determining whether IRCA's assumptions are valid, whether IRCA has met its objectives, and whether policy adjustments in IRCA might be desirable.

III. THE PROGRAM'S FUTURE RESEARCH PROJECTS

While the Program for Research on Immigration Policy will focus on IRCA during the first two years, it nevertheless recognizes that many important immigration issues cannot be addressed within the confines of IRCA. As a consequence, it proposes in future years to address such key questions as:

□ What number and mix of immigrants can best help meet U.S. long-term economic and social interests?
□ What is the relationship between immigration and other policies dealing with the trade of goods and services, capital investments, foreign aid, and national security?
□ What role should public institutions (including schools) and private institutions (including employers) take to facilitate and accelerate the assimilation of immigrants into U.S. society?

To address these kinds of questions, the Program is currently identifying existing data sources and developing effective means for collecting needed data.

IV. PUBLICATIONS AND CONFERENCES

The Program for Research on Immigration Policy will disseminate its findings by publishing a series of papers, reports, and books. To distribute information on IRCA and immigration as broadly as possible, it will also publish annually a document like this one that describes the Program's research, synthesizes and interprets other research, and reports information about current and expected major immigration trends and policy issues.

In addition, the Program convenes working groups and conferences for researchers, policymakers, administrators, and community groups involved with immigration. A Washington, D.C., working group examines national policy issues, and a West Coast working group is looking at regional issues and the operational aspects of the law's implementation. Finally, the Program's first conference was held on May 3, 1989, in Guadalajara, Mexico, to explore the international effects of IRCA, and its second on July 21, 1989, in Washington, D.C., to examine indicators of illegal immigration since the passage of IRCA.

V. ORGANIZATIONAL STRUCTURE

The following figure describes the organizational structure of The Program for Research on Immigration Policy:

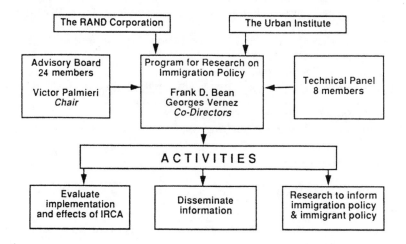

ADVISORY BOARD

The Program's 1988–89 Advisory Board consists of the following members, who represent a broad range of regional, ethnic, and professional perspectives:

Victor H. Palmieri, Chair, The Palmieri Company, New York, NY;
Yvonne Burke, Esq., Jones, Day, Reavis and Pogue, Los Angeles, CA;
Richard Clark, Aspen Institute, Washington, DC;
Richard W. Day, Senate Judiciary Committee, Washington, DC;
Frank P. Del Olmo, Los Angeles Times, Los Angeles, CA;

Arthur P. Endres, Jr., Commission for the Study of International Migration and Cooperative Economic Development, Washington, DC;
Rodrigo Fernandez, Consejo Superior, Universitario Centroamericano, San Jose, Costa Rica;
Marvin E. Frankel, Esq., Kramer, Levin, Nessen, Kamin and Frankel, New York, NY;
Nathan Glazer, Harvard Graduate School of Education, Cambridge, MA;
William Gorham, The Urban Institute, Washington, DC;
Fernando A. Guerra, M.D., San Antonio, TX;
Aileen C. Hernandez, Aileen C. Hernandez Associates, San Francisco, CA;
Warren Leiden, American Immigration Lawyers Association, Washington, DC;
Daniel E. Lungren, Diepenbrock, Wulff, Plant and Hannegan, Sacramento, CA;
David W. Lyon, The RAND Corporation, Santa Monica, CA;
Flora MacDonald, Ottawa, Canada;
F. Ray Marshall, Lyndon Baines Johnson School for Public Affairs, University of Texas, Austin, TX;
Doris Meissner, Carnegie Endowment for International Peace, Washington, DC;
Ambler H. Moss, Jr., Graduate School of International Studies, University of Miami, Coral Gables, FL;
Jose Juan de Olloqui, Banca Serfin, Mexico;
Alejandro Portes, The Johns Hopkins University, Baltimore, MD;
Peter Rodino, Esq., Rodino and Rodino, Washington, DC;
Jean Wente, Wente Brothers, Livermore, CA;
Wilbur Woo, Cathay Bank, Los Angeles, CA.

TECHNICAL ADVISORS

The Program's 1988–89 Panel of Technical Advisors includes the following members:

William Alonso, Center for Population Studies, Harvard University, Cambridge, MA;
Susan E. Berryman, Teachers College, New York, NY;
Michael Greenwood, Department of Economics, University of Colorado, Boulder, CO;
Manuel Garcia y Geiego, El Colegio de Mexico, Mexico City, Mexico;
Ellen P. Kraly, Department of Geography, Colgate University, Hamilton, NY;
Anthony P. Maingot, Department of Political Science, Florida International University, Miami, FL;
Douglas Massey, Population Research Center, University of Chicago, Chicago, IL;
William Armando Vega, Department of Sociology, University of Miami, Coral Gables, FL.

Note

1. An important distinction exists between *immigration policies* and *immigrant policies*. National institutions, such as the Immigration and Naturalization Service, primarily implement and enforce *immigration policies*, which determine the number and characteristics of immigrants allowed to enter and work in the United States. By contrast, public, private, state, and local service delivery agencies primarily implement and enforce *immigrant policies*, which facilitate the social adjustment and entry into the workforce of immigrants once they have come to the United States.

REFERENCES

Auerbach, Frank L., and Elizabeth J. Harper. 1973. *Immigration Laws of the United States*, 2nd ed. Indianapolis: Bobbs-Merrill Co.

Bailyn, Bernard. 1986. *The Peopling of British North America*. New York: Alfred A. Knopf.

Bean, Frank D., and Teresa A. Sullivan. 1985. "Immigration and Its Consequences: Confronting the Problem." *Society*, 22 (May/June): 67–73.

Bean, Frank D., and Marta Tienda. 1988. *The Hispanic Population of the United States*. New York: Russell Sage.

Bean, Frank D., Allan G. King, and Jeffery S. Passel. 1985. "Estimates of the Size of the Illegal Migrant Population of Mexican Origin in the United States: An Assessment, Review and Proposal." In *Mexican Immigrants and Mexican Americans: An Evolving Relation*, edited by H. Browning and R. de la Garza, 13–36. Austin, Tex.: Center for Mexican American Studies.

Bean, Frank D., B. Lindsay Lowell, and Lowell J. Taylor. 1988. "Undocumented Mexican Immigrants and the Earnings of Other Workers in the United States." *Demography*, 25(1, February): 35–52.

Bean, Frank D., Edward E. Telles, and B. Lindsay Lowell. 1987. "Undocumented Migration to the United States: Perception and Evidence." *Population and Development Review*, 13(4, December): 671–690.

Bean, Frank D., Jurgen Schmandt, and Sidney Weintraub, eds. 1989. *Mexican and Central American Population and U.S. Immigration Policy*. Austin, Tex: Center for Mexican American Studies and University of Texas Press.

Bennett, Marion T. 1963. *American Immigration Policies: A History*. New York: Public Affairs Press.

Borjas, George J., and Marta Tienda. 1987. "The Economic Consequences of Immigration," *Science*, 235(February 6): 645–651.

Bruening, Tom. 1988. "Foreign Agricultural Workers and Farm Labor." In *In Defense of the Alien*, edited by Lydio F. Tomasi. Vol. 10, 74–77. New York: Center for Migration Studies.

Cafferty, Pastora San Juan, Barry R. Chiswick, Andrew M. Greenley, and Teresa A. Sullivan. 1983. *The Dilemma of American Immigration: Beyond the Golden Door*. New Brunswick, N.J.: Transaction.

Cardoza-Fonseca v. INS. 480 U.S. 421, 107 S.Ct. 1207 (1987).

Carrasco, Gilbert Paul. 1988. "The Golden Moment of Legalization." In *In Defense of the Alien*, edited by Lydio F. Tomasi. Vol. 10, 32–49. New York: Center for Migration Studies.

Chavez, Leo R. 1988. "Settlers and Sojourners: The Case of Mexicans in the United States." *Human Organization*, 47 (2, Summer): 95–107.

CHIRLA. See Coalition for Humane Immigration Rights of Los Angeles.

Coalition for Humane Immigration Rights of Los Angeles. 1988. "Preliminary Report: The Effects of Employer Sanctions on Workers." Los Angeles: Monograph, October 13.

Cornelius, Wayne. 1988. "The Persistence of Immigrant-Dominated Firms and Industries in the United States: The Case of California." Paper prepared for the Conference on Comparative Migration Studies, Paris, June.

Divine, Robert A. 1957. *American Immigration Policy, 1924–1952*. New Haven: Yale University Press.

DOL. See U.S. Department of Labor.

Espenshade, Thomas J. 1989. "Growing Imbalances Between Labor Supply and Labor Demand in the Caribbean Basin." In *Mexican and Central American Population and U.S. Immigration Policy*, edited by Frank D. Bean, Jurgen Schmandt and Sidney Weintraub, Austin, Tex.: Center for Mexican American Studies and University of Texas Press.

Espenshade, Thomas J., et al. 1988. "Immigration Policy in the United States: Future Prospects for the Immigration Reform and Control Act of 1986." Working Paper, PRIP–UI–2. Washington, D.C.: Urban Institute, October.

Freeman, Richard B., ed. 1988. *NBER Summary Report: Immigration, Trade, and the Labor Market*. Cambridge, Mass.: National Bureau of Economic Research.

Fuchs, Lawrence H. 1987. "The Corpse that Would Not Die: The Immigration Reform and Control Act of 1986." Paper presented at the American Political Science Convention, Chicago, Sept. 3–6.

———. Forthcoming. "The Blood of All Nations: The Triumph of Inclusivity in Immigration Policy." *Ethnicity and Public Policy*, 7 (1990).

GAO. See U.S. General Accounting Office.

Haitian Refugee Center v. Nelson (S.D. Fla., August 22, 1988).

Hernandez v. Meese (E.D. Cal., March 25, 1988).

Higham, John. 1985. *Strangers in the Land*. New Brunswick, N.J.: Rutgers University Press.

Hoefer, Michael D. 1988a. "An Interim Report on Aliens Legalizing under IRCA." Paper prepared for the annual meeting of the Population Association of America, New Orleans, April 20–23.

———. 1988b. "Background of U.S. Immigration Policy Reform." Paper prepared for Rutgers University Colloquium on "U.S. Immigration Policy Reform," New Brunswick, N.J., October 14.

Hutchinson, Edward P. 1981. *Legislative History of American Immigration Policy, 1798–1985*. Philadelphia: University of Pennsylvania Press.

INS. See U.S. Immigration and Naturalization Service.

IRCA. See U.S. Congress. Immigration Reform and Control Act of 1986.

Jasso, G., and M. R. Rosenzweig. 1986. "Family Reunification and the Immigration Multiplier: U.S. Immigration Law, Origin–Country Conditions, and the Reproduction of Immigrants." Demography, 23: 291–312.

Keely, Charles B. 1982. "Illegal Immigration," Scientific American, 246(March): 4–7.

Lamm, Richard D., and Gary Imhoff. 1985. The Immigration Time Bomb. New York: Truman Talley Books.

Levine, David B., Kenneth Hill, and Robert Warren, eds. 1985. Immigration Statistics: A Story of Neglect. Washington, D.C.: National Academy Press.

Martin, Philip L., and J. Edward Taylor. 1988. "Harvest of Confusion: SAWs, RAWs, and Farmworkers." Working Paper PRIP-VI-4. Washington, D.C.: Urban Institute, December.

Massey, Douglas S., Rafael Alarcon, Jorge Durand, and Humberto Gonzales. 1987. Return to Aztlan: The Social Process of International Migration from Western Mexico. Berkeley: University of California Press.

Mathews, Jay. 1988. "Using Fake Papers, Migrants Skirt Law." Washington Post, November 3, Section A, 3.

McCarthy, Kevin F., and R. Burciaga Valdez. 1986. Current and Future Effects of Mexican Immigration in California. Santa Monica, CA: Rand, May.

Meissner, Doris M., and Demetrios G. Papademetriou. 1988. The Legalization Countdown: A Third-Quarter Assessment. Washington, D.C.: Carnegie Endowment for International Peace, February.

Merino, Catherine L. 1988. "Compromising Immigration Reform: The Creation of a Vulnerable Subclass." Yale Law Journal, 98(2, December): 409–426.

Muller, Thomas, and Thomas T. Espenshade. 1985. The Fourth Wave: California's Newest Immigrants. Washington D.C.: Urban Institute Press.

National Council of La Raza. 1988. "Policy Memorandum on the Status of the Immigration Reform and Control Act of 1986." Washington, D.C.: National Council of La Raza. November 4.

New York State Inter-Agency Task Force on Immigration Affairs. 1988. Workplace Discrimination under the Immigration Reform and Control Act of 1986: A Study of the Impacts on New Yorkers. Albany, NY: New York State Inter-Agency Task Force on Immigration Affairs. November 4.

North, David S., and Anna Mary Portz. 1988. "Through the Maze: An Interim Report on the Alien Legalization Program." Washington, D.C.: TransCentury Development Associates. March 28.

Norton, Richard E. 1988. "INS and Legalization." In In Defense of the Alien, edited by Lydio F. Tomasi. Vol. 10, 23–27. New York: Center for Migration Studies.

NuStats, Inc. 1987. *Baseline Study of Hispanic Illegal Residents: Narrative Summary.* Conducted for the Justice Group on behalf of the INS, U.S. Department of Justice. Austin, Tex: NuStats, Inc. September.

NYS. See New York State Inter-Agency Task Force on Immigration Affairs.

Orantes-Hernandez v. Smith. 541 F. Supp. 351 (C.D. Cal. 1982).

Passel, Jeffrey S. 1986. "Undocumented Immigration." *The Annals,* 487(September): 181–121.

The President's Comprehensive Triennial Report on Immigration. 1989. Prepared by the Executive Branch. Washington, D.C.: U.S. Government Printing Office. May.

Reimers, David M. 1985. *Still the Golden Door: The Third World Comes to America.* New York: Columbia University Press.

Rosenberg, Howard R., and John W. Mamer. 1987. "The Impact of the New Immigration Reform Act." *California Agriculture,* 41 (March–April): 30–32.

Schroeder, John R. 1988. "The Immigration Reform and Control Act of 1986." In *In Defense of the Alien,* edited by Lydio F. Tomasi. Vol. 10, 3–9. New York: Center for Migration Studies.

State of California, Employment Development Department. 1988. *California Looks at the U.S. Immigration Reform and Control Act,* Sacramento: April.

Stein, Dan. 1989. *The Immigration Act of 1989.* Testimony before the Subcommittee on Immigration and Refugee Affairs, Committee on the Judiciary, U.S. Senate, concerning Proposed Legislation, S.358. 101st Cong, 1st Sess., March 3.

Suro, Roberto. 1989. "1986 Amnesty Law is Seen as Failing to Slow Alien Tide." *New York Times,* June 18, Section 1, 1.

Taylor, J. Edward. 1986. *U.S. Immigration Policy, the Mexican Village Economy, and Agricultural Labor Markets in California.* Final report to the National Center for Food and Agricultural Policy, Resources for the Future. Washington, D.C.: The Urban Institute. September.

U.S. Congress. House Subcommittee on Immigration, Refugees, and International Law, Committee on the Judiciary. 1984. *Temporary Suspension of Deportation of Certain Aliens: Hearing.* 97th Cong., 2nd Sess., April 12, 109.

————. 1986. *Immigration Reform and Control Act of 1986.* PL 99–603, S.1200, November 6.

U.S. Department of Labor. 1988. *Implementation of the Temporary Agricultural Worker Program (H–2A).* Report from the President to Congress, Washington, D.C.: U.S. Immigration and Naturalization Service, November.

U.S. General Accounting Office. 1987a. *Illegal Aliens: Extent of Problems Experienced by Returned Salvadorans Not Determinable.* GAO/

NSSIAD-87-158BR. Washington, D.C.: U.S. Government Printing Office, May.

————. 1987b. *Immigration Reform: Systematic Alien Verification System Could Be Improved.* GAO/IMTEC-87-45BR. Washington, D.C.: U.S. Government Printing Office, September.

————. 1987c. *Immigration Reform: Verifying the Status of Aliens Applying for Federal Benefits.* GAO/HRD-88-7. Washington, D.C.: U.S. Government Printing Office, October 1.

————. 1987d. *Immigration Reform: Status of Implementing Employer Sanctions after One Year.* GAO/GGD-88-14. Washington, D.C.: U.S. Government Printing Office, November.

————. 1988a. *Immigration: The Future Flow of Legal Immigration to the U.S.* GAO/PEMD-88-7. Washington, D.C.: U.S. Government Printing Office, January.

————. 1988b. *Immigration: Studies of the Immigration Control Act's Impact on Mexico.* GAO/NSIAD-88-92BR. Washington, D.C.: U.S. Government Printing Office, February.

————. 1988c. *The H–2A Program: Protections for U.S. Farmworkers.* GAO/PEMD-89-3. Washington, D.C.: U.S. Government Printing Office, October.

————. 1988d. *Immigration Control: A New Role for the Social Security Card.* GAO-HRD-88-4. Washington, D.C.: U.S. Government Printing Office, March.

————. 1988e. *Immigration Reform: Status of Implementing Employer Sanctions after Second Year.* GAO/GGD-89-16. Washington, D.C.: U.S. Government Printing Office, November.

U.S. Immigration and Naturalization Service. 1983. *1982 Statistical Yearbook of the Immigration and Naturalization Service.* Washington, D.C.: U.S. Department of Justice.

————. 1984. *1983 Statistical Yearbook of the Immigration and Naturalization Service.* Washington, D.C.: U.S. Department of Justice.

————. 1987. "1987 Unpublished Data on Asylum cases Filed with District Directors, Fiscal Year 1987." Washington, D.C.: Statistics Division, U.S. Immigration and Naturalization Service, September.

————. 1988a. *1987 Statistical Yearbook of the Immigration and Naturalization Service.* Washington, D.C.: U.S. Department of Justice.

————. 1988b. "Provisional Legalization Application Statistics." Washington, D.C.: Statistics Division, U.S. Immigration and Naturalization Service, January 8.

————. 1988c. "1988 Unpublished Data on Asylum cases Filed with District Directors, Fiscal Year 1988." Washington, D.C.: Statistics Division, U.S. Immigration and Naturalization Service, March.

————. 1989a. "Provisional Legalization Application Statistics." Washington, D.C.: Statistics Division, U.S. Immigration and Naturalization Service, January 27.

————. 1989b. *Immigration Statistics: Fiscal Year 1988.* Washington, D.C.:

Statistics Division, U.S. Immigration and Naturalization Service, April.

U.S. Office of Management and Budget. 1986. *Appendix to the Budget of the U.S. Government FY 1987.* Washington, D.C.: U.S. Government Printing Office.

————. 1987. *Appendix to the Budget of the U.S. Government FY 1988.* Washington, D.C.: U.S. Government Printing Office.

————. 1988. *Appendix to the Budget of the U.S. Government FY 1989.* Washington, D.C.: U.S. Government Printing Office.

————. 1989. *Appendix to the Budget of the U.S. Government FY 1990.* Washington, D.C.: U.S. Government Printing Office.

U.S. Select Commission on Immigration and Refugee Policy. 1981. *U.S. Immigration Policy and the National Interest: The Staff Report of The Select Commission on Immigration and Refugee Policy.* Washington, D.C.: U.S. Government Printing Office.

Villafranca, Armando. 1988. "Refugees Strain Valley INS Office: Central Americans Seek Political Asylum." *Corpus Cristi Caller-Times,* November 18, A-1.

Warren, Robert, and J. M. Peck. 1980. "Foreign-born Emigration to the U.S.: 1960–1970." *Demography,* 17: 71–84.

Warren, Robert and Jeffrey S. Passel. 1987. "A Count of the Uncountable: Estimates of Undocumented Aliens Counted in the 1980 U.S. Census." *Demography,* 24: 375–96.

Zucker, Norman L. and Naomi Flink Zucker. 1987. *The American Gate: The Reality of American Refugee Policy.* San Diego: Harcourt Brace Jovanovich.

ABOUT THE AUTHORS

Frank D. Bean is codirector of the Program for Research on Immigration Policy and Director of the Population Studies Center at The Urban Institute. He has written extensively on topics dealing with racial and ethnic group demography and with immigration issues, including *The Hispanic Population of the United States* (with Marta Tienda) and *Mexican and Central American Population and U.S. Immigration Policy* (edited with Sidney Weintraub and Jurgen Schmandt).

Georges Vernez is codirector of the Program for Research on Immigration Policy and Director of the Education and Human Resources Program at the RAND Corporation. A policy analyst with expertise in immigration, human resources, organization and management, and urban and economic development, he has written on numerous topics in these areas.

Charles B. Keely is the Donald G. Herzberg Professor of International Migration in the Department of Demography and the Center for Immigration Policy and Refugee Assistance at Georgetown University. An expert on international migration and immigration policy, he has published *U.S. Immigration: A Policy Analysis* and *Global Trends in Migration* (edited with Mary Kritz and S. M. Tomasi).